The Simpson Xavier Guide to

THE
FAMILY BUSINESS
IN IRELAND

Philip Smyth FCA
and
Peter C. Leach FCA

SIMPSON XAVIER
Chartered Accountants
A member of Horwath International

BLACKWATER PRESS

This Irish edition published in 1993 by

Blackwater Press
8 Airton Road
Tallaght
Dublin 24

ISBN: 0 86121 487 0

Editor
Anna O'Donovan

Consultant Editor
Simon Perry

First published in the UK in 1991 by Kogan Page Ltd, London

© Stoy Hayward, 1991

This guide has been prepared with the aim of providing the business person with an overview of family business in Ireland. In relation to company and taxation matters the text does not purport to be an exhaustive interpretation of the law in Ireland. The authors and Simpson Xavier accept no liability for anyone who relies solely on the material contained in this guide.

We strongly recommend that if anyone wishes to pursue seriously any of the courses outlined in the guide that they should contact their professional advisers or Simpson Xavier.

Contents

Acknowledgements

First of all, we would like to thank our colleagues David Clancy, Paul Keenan, Wendy Kenway-Smith, Fi Inchbald and Jenny Lacey for their help in the preparation of this book. The cartoons were drawn by Sandy Peters, and the charts by PanTec Arts.

In the footnotes throughout the book we have drawn attention to various published sources of valuable information and analysis on family-owned businesses. These footnotes, however, are confined to highlighting direct references to, or quotations from, such sources that feature in the text. In addition, we would like to mention here a number of other published studies and papers that, although not directly quoted in the book, have constituted essential background reading.

In particular, we would like to acknowledge an important source of US information and ideas – *Your Family Business: A Success Guide for Growth and Survival* (Benson, Crego, and Drucker), published in 1990 by Dow Jones-Irwin Inc. The book represents the standard reference on family business-related issues from a US perspective, and we would recommend it to any readers interested in undertaking further research on this subject.

Another interesting source is, 'Family Business: Perspectives on Change', *The Wharton Annual, 1984*, by Peter Davis. This article analyses the confusion between personal and professional life within family businesses. Peter Davis is probably the world's leading authority on family businesses and all his published work on the subject provides stimulating reading. Many of his ideas are discussed in the following text and it is fair to say that, without his inspiration and support, this book might well not have seen the light of day.

Further useful sources include: *Secrets of Success*, Sidgwick and Jackson, 1988, by Clive Rassam; 'Marrying into a Family Business', *Nation's Business, April 1989*, by Sharon Nelton (discusses coping with the problems that can arise when marriage brings an 'outsider' into the family); and 'Human Resource Management in the Family-owned Company', *Journal of General Management, Spring 1980*, by Robert Dailey and Thomas Reuschling (the results of valuable research on the family factors that disrupt standard human resource practices).

Last, but by no means least, we gratefully acknowledge the contributions of our wives, Cora Smyth and Antonia Leach. Their advice, enthusiasm and patience during the preparation of this book has been invaluable.

Foreword
by Sir John Harvey-Jones MBE

It would be difficult to overestimate the crucial importance of the success of our family businesses to the well-being of every citizen in the country.

We urgently need to create more wealth and to have a more internationally competitive and successful business base in this country if we are to achieve the many social and personal objectives that are so widely shared.

Family businesses comprise over 90 per cent of all the businesses in Ireland and it has been estimated that over 50 per cent of people employed are employed in family businesses. On that level alone, without considering the national interests, it is amazing that we have lagged so greatly in providing the background of support and help for these businesses, which is more readily available in the UK, America and on the Continent.

I believe partly the reason for this is that we have tended to lump together family businesses as a generic term with small businesses, but only a moment's reflection is needed to show that they are widely different, both in their strengths and opportunities, and in their problems.

As far as the problems are concerned it is difficult enough to manage an entire family's personal, intricate relationships well. Most of us only get one chance at doing this and are, so to speak, learning on the run. Managing our family involves ensuring that every one of us grows, that we have shared objectives, that we have the mutuality of support we tend to take for granted, and so on. Managing a business is no easier, as the many business failures and the relatively short life of most business organisations will testify.

It is indeed no accident that a disproportionate number of the businesses which have survived longest are, or have been, family businesses, where the nearly impossible task of running the family's objectives and the firm's objectives in harness has been achieved. It seems to me abundantly clear that family businesses have all the problems of running a business, with an extra overlay of specific and different problems which have to be managed to boot.

It was only the making of the *Troubleshooter* series that made me, for the first time, stop and realise the unique nature of the skills required in running a family business. In that series, behind every business problem lay a family drama, and in most cases the one could only be resolved satisfactorily by attacking the other.

It was a surprise to me therefore to find how little work had been done in this area, and that almost all the thinking had been produced outside Ireland. There is evidence that family businesses in Ireland have different objectives and different patterns of behaviour from family businesses elsewhere. This may be partly because of the different fiscal environment, or possibly partly due to the differences in family life between Ireland and other countries. While, therefore, the research and work that has been done elsewhere is probably relevant, I doubt whether it can be transferred in totality to Ireland.

As well as their sheer numbers, family businesses contribute a disproportionate share to our social stability and economic success in this country. They are able to, and do, take a longer-term view than many publicly quoted companies, and they are also able to apply consistency of aim and stability in a business environment which, within public companies, tends increasingly to feel more like a zig-zag than a steady progression.

I therefore welcome this book by Philip Smyth and Peter Leach, on behalf of Simpson Xavier, which is one of the very few organisations that has sought specifically to help and become involved with the furtherance of family businesses in Ireland.

Commentary
by Fergal Quinn

Was it St. Munchin who said, 'Rags to riches and back to rags in three generations'? If so, he is probably out of date now. In a highly competitive world, a successful business will not last even three decades unless it is well looked after. This book gives a range of pointers to help the family business to survive, not just the three decades but the three generations too.

It examines critically and usefully many of the questions that family businesses need to ask. Asking questions about a business is the first step. Finding answers to these questions is further along the road. Philip Smyth and Peter Leach offer a number of alternative solutions to each question – and some of those solutions might not have crossed the minds of the questioners. Should the founder risk the family business by promoting a family member ahead of the most professional manager? Of course not, we say, but over and over again we see that behaviour does not reflect good intentions.

Farming may not always have been regarded as a 'business', but there is no doubt that in Ireland, in the last decade of the 20th century, the Irish family farm will need to be run as a business if it is to survive into the 21st century.

'Do not overlook daughters' is one of the section headings in Chapter 7 on 'Succession management' and it is a heading that is a particularly useful reminder in Ireland, whether the business is a farm, a shop or a manufacturer. Some of Ireland's most successful family businesses represent examples of enterprises that did not overlook women.

This book is welcome in Ireland, and if it just starts the debate on the importance of the family business it will have done well. Our Constitution exalts the family as a unit, but our laws – both fiscal and economic – have tended to ignore the importance of family business. I hope this book will help redress the balance.

Preface

With the transition from enterprise culture to an economy in recession, family firms are facing increasingly complex issues which affect not only the destiny of the business itself, but also those of the proprietor, his family, and his employees.

How does the proprietor reconcile his own and his family's aspirations with the commercial goals of the firm? Can he motivate family and non-family employees alike? Should he try to solve problems himself, or should he take independent advice? The major issue of who is to succeed him – when should he start planning succession and who should he choose? Other matters include whether to sell out, raise external finance, diversify, merge, bring in more family members or more outside management, and so on.

All these dilemmas affect most family businesses sooner or later, yet there is virtually no written guidance for proprietors to help them make the right decisions. Very often, by the time the problems associated with the issues arise, it is too late to take action and the business is on the brink of failure. The chances of success for a family business are greatly increased by ensuring the major, life-threatening questions are tackled at an early stage and plans developed for the future. In the same way that, for example, the future of the company's operations has to be continually examined, new avenues explored and decisions made, the development of the firm's relationship with the family needs to be constantly assessed and reviewed.

Proprietors often fail to consider this subject in sufficient detail. Too involved with the day-to-day activities of their company, they put off getting to grips with these vital questions until a later date. Reluctance to face the problems and to take external professional advice often stems from the proprietor's inability to gain knowledge himself about the difficulties and the forces that are at work. How, for example, have others tackled the problems and with what consequences for the firm? What, in fact, may happen if the issue is ignored – will it go away or will a major crisis arise?

This book is therefore intended as a guide for those involved in a family business, or who are contemplating joining one, to help them identify and resolve the family-related issues that are potentially so destructive. By recognising and dealing with these questions early, the commercial requirements of the business will not be disrupted by the family involvement, and a well-equipped, healthy company can be passed on to the next generation.

The book is organised into three parts. Part I (especially Chapters 1 and 2) concentrates on explaining the unique dynamics of family businesses, why they are different from non-family firms, and the advantages and disadvantages that flow from their special status. Each family member (the owner, owner's spouse, children, cousins, and so on) have a different perspective on the business, and understanding their individual viewpoints is a key ingredient in the successful management of family-owned companies.

Chapter 3 discusses the common characteristics of strong families and examines the principal causes of family conflict – the difficulties that can arise in father–son relationships and sibling rivalry. Various strategies for getting to grips with these problems are evaluated, and the chapter goes on to emphasise the critical importance of developing a family strategic plan to ensure a cohesive, family approach to the business.

Part II is devoted to discussing ways of trying to free the business from the restrictive and inhibiting aspects of family involvement. This principally relates to professionalising the firm's operations and, in Chapter 4, the fundamental requirements of effective organisational change are identified, accompanied by an explanation of the main ingredients of planning, organising, staffing, and controlling. Chapters 5 and 6 concentrate on human resources in the family-owned business. Techniques are described that help to disentangle psychological and emotional family issues in the key areas of recruitment, remuneration, performance appraisal, and motivation. At the senior level, the value of independent advisers

and non-family board members is highlighted, as well as the role
non-executive directors can play in bringing a new, and often much
needed, injection of objectivity and experience to board deliberations.

Part III, entitled 'The Next Generation', aims to tackle the
difficult and emotionally charged issues of management and
ownership succession. Chapter 7 tries to help family business
people understand and cope with management succession. It
examines all the options, explains the importance of preparation
and planning, and provides practical guidelines on ensuring that
the transition is accomplished as advantageously and as smoothly
as possible. Chapter 8 addresses the children's perspective on
succession. It examines how children should prepare for entry into
the family business, the importance of negotiating the right entry
deal, and how they should handle their relationships with
non-family employees as well as with the owner-manager.

Chapter 9 concerns the situation where the owner wants to exit
from the business during his lifetime. Here, therefore, the discussion centres on building financial security for the owner and
how this can be achieved in a tax-efficient way. It also covers the
often emotive subject of selling the business, including guidance
on valuation, negotiation, selling to the children or to outsiders,
and going public.

If the business is to remain in family hands beyond the lifetime
of the owners, careful planning is needed to transfer share
ownership into the right hands in the next generation, without
incurring crippling inheritance tax liabilities. Chapter 10 deals
with the issues which surround this transfer, exploring the
emotional, tax and other financial implications from the owner's
point of view, and the effect on the next generation.

In writing the book, we have resisted the temptation to include
a lot of short case histories and anecdotes within chapters in order
to illustrate the experiences of particular Irish companies in
relation to individual points discussed in the text. We felt that to
do this would often distract attention away from key chapter
themes and, more importantly, would create a false impression
that there are hard and fast rules which must be adhered to in
particular cases. On the contrary, one of the main messages of the
book is that there are certain guiding principles that can be flexibly
applied in a variety of family business situations. Case histories

have therefore been grouped together at the end of Parts I, II and III of the book, and illustrate some of the main suggestions and problem-solving techniques discussed in the preceding text.

Finally, unless otherwise indicated, we have used the masculine pronoun throughout this book. This stems from a desire to avoid using ugly and cumbersome language, and no discrimination, prejudice, or bias is intended.

Philip Smyth and Peter C. Leach
August, 1993

PART I

THE ENTREPRENEUR AND THE FAMILY

1 Family Business Dynamics

Family businesses differ in a variety of critically important ways from non-family businesses, and business families function quite differently from non-business families. These two types of distinction lie at the heart of this book and, if a family business is to achieve its full potential, it is vital that its management understands them and the challenges they create. As well as making the right decisions on the commercial problems which beset all enterprises, family businesses have to be able to analyse the special dynamics that surround the founder, the family, the firm and the future. They need to develop special skills that enable them to identify and resolve the unique difficulties which these dynamics introduce, and to adopt constructive strategies to foster growth of the business and the transfer of power and control within it.

So understanding the characteristics that distinguish family and non-family businesses and entrepreneurial and 'normal' families is the first step, and highlighting these distinctions is the main aim of this chapter. However, it should not be concluded from this that there are any general panaceas: every family business is idiosyncratic, shaped by its own set of distinctive personalities, their concerns, objectives and relationships, as well as by a host of other personal and commercial characteristics. But there are some common patterns of experience, and developing an appreciation of them is important so we can avoid repeating everyone else's mistakes.

Before looking at some of the types of commercial activity in which family businesses have proved especially successful, it is important to make clear at the outset what is meant by a 'family business'. Criteria which are too rigid should be avoided – just looking at share ownership or management composition often leads to an inadequate picture and the wrong conclusions. In this book, therefore, a family business is one which, quite simply, is influenced by a family or by a family relationship. In the clearest example, the family as a body may effectively control business operations because it owns more than 50 per cent of the voting shares, or because family members fill a significant number of the top management positions. But as well as these cases, the less obvious situation should not be overlooked where a firm's operations are affected by a family relationship – enterprises in which the relationship of father and son, brother and sister, in-laws, cousins and so on have an important impact on the future of the business. The role of the family in the family business needs to be better understood if the strengths of family businesses are to be maximised and their weaknesses controlled or eliminated.

FAMILY BUSINESS SECTORS

Although family firms are to be found in every sector of Irish commercial activity, their special strengths mean that they flourish best in fields in which their advantages can be fully exploited (see Table 1.1).

Table 1.1 *Prosperous sectors for family businesses*

• Owner-manager
• Service industries
• Entrepreneurial
• Cash rich
• Niche/knowledge-based
• Supply/distribution

Thus, family businesses tend to do well in sectors in which the owner-manager feature is important, particularly in the service industries; for example, most hotel chains in Ireland and indeed throughout the world are still family owned. Family firms are also found in activities where entrepreneurial drive remains a key ingredient of success in the business; there is a great tradition in the retail sector, for instance, of businesses being passed on from one generation to the next.

An above average representation of family businesses is to be found in sectors where cash flow is good. Cash is critically important in the financing of family companies and an examination of the history of industrial development highlights, for example, food processing, which has traditionally been a good cash generator, with long-established companies such as Cadbury-Schweppes in the UK and Heinz and Campbell Soups in the US, all still in family hands. This situation is in marked contrast to Ireland where the sector is largely controlled by the co-ops. Similarly, family businesses tend to do well in niche sectors, often still trading on the genius of someone who founded the company many years ago, or where the business is based on some specific knowledge or trading secret that represents the key to success.

Finally, family businesses are relatively successful in supply industries where the business involves supply relationships with other larger companies that appreciate and value the owner presence. Thus a lot of family businesses are distributorships, especially in the motor sector.

THE SPECIAL STRENGTHS
AND WEAKNESSES OF FAMILY FIRMS

It is easy to underestimate the size and importance of the family business sector. The success of those involved in managing family businesses determines the performance of the major portion of Irish commercial activity. These managers have a number of family business-related advantages working in their favour, but at the same time they must face up to and battle with a range of serious problems and drawbacks. Let's examine the plus points first.

The advantages

The overriding characteristic that distinguishes most family businesses is a unique atmosphere which creates a 'sense of belonging' and an enhanced common purpose among the whole work-force. Although intangible, this factor manifests itself in a number of very concrete and positive attributes that can serve to give family businesses a significant competitive edge. These are summarised in Table 1.2, but it is worth examining them in detail.

Commitment

People who set up a business can become very passionate about it – it is their creation, they nurtured it, built it up and, for many such entrepreneurs, their business is their life. This very deep affection translates naturally into dedication and commitment, which extends to all the family members who come to have a stake in the success of the business. They feel they have a family responsibility to pull together and, provided there are no conflicts, everyone is happy to put in far more time and energy working for the company's success than they would dream of devoting to a normal job. Family enthusiasm develops added commitment and loyalty from their work-forces – people care

Table 1.2 *What makes family businesses good?*

• Commitment
• Knowledge
• Flexibility in time, work and money
• Long-range thinking
• A stable culture
• Speedy decision making
• Reliability and pride

more and feel they are part of a team, all contributing to the common purpose.

Knowledge

Family businesses often have particular ways of doing things – special technological or commercial know-how not possessed by their competitors; knowledge which would soon become general in a normal commercial environment, but which can be coveted and protected within the family.

This idea of knowledge is also relevant in relation to the founder's sons or daughters joining the business. Children grow up learning about the business, infected by the founder's enthusiasm, and when the time comes for them to join they may already have a very deep understanding of what the business is all about.

Flexibility in work, time and money

Essentially this factor boils down to putting the work and time into the business which is necessary, and taking out money when you can afford to. A further aspect of commitment is that if work needs to be done and time spent in developing the business, then the family puts in the time and does the work – there is no negotiating of overtime rates or special bonuses for a rushed job.

The same flexibility applies concerning money, and here lies another important distinction between entrepreneurial and non-business families. Most families have a set income derived from wages or salaries paid by an employer, and the only decisions the family take concern how this income is to be spent. But for families in business, income is not a fixed element in the domestic equation: they must decide how much money they can safely take from the business for their own needs while at the same time preserving the firm's financial flexibility and its scope for investment. Sometimes, one aspect of commitment to the family business takes the form of total horror at the idea of removing money from it – 'draining the business of its life-blood' can be how the family see it, even if the business has been trading profitably for decades. So you find examples of some of Ireland's wealthiest families who, quite literally, do not have any ready money because their company, often established generations ago, has never paid a dividend. All its profits have been re-invested to finance future growth.

Flexibility in time, work and money once again leads to a competitive advantage for family businesses. They can adapt quickly and easily to changing circumstances. If, for example, the firm needs to switch into a new product to capitalise on a developing trend in the market-place, the decision will rarely involve lengthy discussion by a hierarchy of committees, and its implementation will be equally speedy – 'we are going to stop doing this, start doing that, and the move will mean we have to put in six months of extra hard work and not take any money out of the business for the next two years'. A tall order for many companies, impossible for others, but a typical, flexible agenda for a lot of family businesses.

Long-range thinking
Family businesses tend to be better than other enterprises at thinking long term. Strategic planning reduces risk, enables a business to cope more effectively with unforeseen events, and is also the hallmark of a great many successful new ventures and of long-term survivors. The fact that families usually have a quite clear view of their commercial objectives across, say, the next 10 or 15 years, can therefore represent a considerable advantage.

Dr. Peter Davis of Wharton Business School, one of the leading authorities on family-owned business issues, regards this feature of family businesses as potentially very important:

> When you think about it, if there is any entity in our economy that can match the philosophy which the Japanese have introduced into the business world in the last 15 years, it is family businesses. The quick-hit capitalist cannot do it, and publicly traded companies cannot do it because they are concerned about quarterly or half-yearly earnings. The

privately held family business is the only entity that can truly build for the long run.[1]

But although families are good at thinking long term, they are not so good at formalising their plans – writing them down, analysing the assumptions they are making, testing past results against earlier predictions – in short, the strength means that the long-range thinking is there, while the weakness is that this thinking is undisciplined. If the right environment exists for a family to build on its vision of the future and to focus on and get behind the type of long-term strategic intent which has characterised Japanese business, then the possibilities are immense. Strategic planning will be discussed in detail in Chapter 4, especially in relation to ways in which the family's strategic plan can be integrated into that of the business.

A stable culture

For a variety of reasons, family businesses tend to be stable structures. The chairman or managing director has usually been around for many years and the key management personnel are all committed to the success of the business and they too are there for the long term. Relationships within the company have usually had ample time to develop and stabilise, as have the company's procedural ethics and working practices – everybody knows how things are done.

Like some of the other factors working in favour of family businesses, however, a strong, stable culture can be a two-edged sword. A very stable business environment can become a dangerously introverted atmosphere in which the attitude is, 'We do it this way because we have always done it this way', and nobody is thinking about change and looking to see if doing things differently might mean that they are done more efficiently. So stability in the family business is one of its unique

---

[1]Presentation at the *Your family business in the 1990s and beyond* seminar,. London, 3rd May, 1990.

and valuable assets; but at the same time some thought needs to be given to whether a stable business culture has in fact become an obstacle to change and adaptability.

Speedy decisions

In a family-controlled business, responsibilities are usually very clearly defined and the decision-making process is deliberately restricted to one or two key individuals. In many cases this means that if you want the company to do something you go and ask the boss and the boss will either say 'yes' or 'no'.

The contrast with this process is at its most stark if one looks at the example of a public company deciding to shift its operations into new trading areas. If the decision is likely to change the shape of the business significantly then it will involve rather more than a 'yes' or 'no' from the boss. Typically, the process will begin with an 'in principle' board decision to investigate the move, feasibility studies will be undertaken which will then be examined by specially appointed board committees, the company's banking, accounting and legal advisers will all become involved in the process, a board decision will be taken to approve the move, but even then shareholder approval may have to be sought via a lengthy and elaborately detailed circular designed to summarise the arguments and quantify the financial impact of the change. Of course, this is not to say that advice from outsiders on important decisions is a waste of time, or that the consequences of such a major move should not be extremely carefully evaluated. But speed does have a commercial value and, in this example, if a lot rested on the speed with which a decision could be taken and implemented, then the family business would definitely have the edge.

Reliability and pride

Commitment and a stable culture lie behind the fact that family businesses are generally very solid and reliable structures – and are perceived as such in the market-place. Many customers prefer doing business with a firm which has been established for a long time, and they will have tended to build up relationships with a management and staff that is not constantly changing jobs within the firm or being replaced by outsiders. Also, the commitment within the family business, discussed earlier, is not just a hidden force – it reveals itself to customers all the time in the form of a friendlier, more knowledgeable, more skilful and generally much higher standard of service and customer care.

Closely connected with reliability is the notion of pride: the people who run family businesses are generally extremely proud of the business, proud of their achievement in having established and built it, and their staff are proud to be associated with the family and what they are doing. This pride, which in some circumstances can tend to almost institutionalise the business, is often translated into a powerful marketing tool. So Cooper's Ale in Australia advertise their beers with the slogan, 'Taste the difference that four generations of brewing tradition makes'; similarly, there is a preserve maker in the north-east of England which stamps its jam pot labels with, 'The difference is our family pride'; Brennan's Bread advertise their products with the slogan, 'Old Mr. Brennan, etc ....'; and Harry Moore starts a radio advertisement with the words, 'For more years than I care to remember ....'

Myth or reality?

Because of the often anecdotal flavour of some of these advantages enjoyed by family businesses, in 1992 a study was undertaken in the UK[2] to test out whether such factors as commitment, stability, flexibility, long-term planning, and so on, actually translate into tangible commercial returns. In other words, do family businesses really have an edge on their non-family business competitors?

In conjunction with BBC2's *Business Matters* series, Stoy

---

[2]Stoy Hayward/BBC (1992). *The Stoy Hayward / BBC Family Business Index: A Report.*

Hayward examined the performance of family public companies listed on the UK stock exchange. The study identified, via share registers, a total of 71 companies that had been listed on the stock exchange since 31st December, 1970 and in which a family, or family interests, controlled at least 25 per cent of the ordinary share capital. These companies comprise the 'Family Business Index'.

The market capitalisation of Index companies varied from around £1 million to nearly £200 million, with approximately 70 per cent of firms in the sample capitalised in the range £1 million to £15 million. Share price information was obtained (adjusted for share splits, rights issues, etc, but excluding dividend payments) for the period 31st December, 1970 to 31st December, 1991.

The study results showed that £1 invested in the FT All Share Index at the end of 1970 would have grown to £8.72 at 31st December, 1991. In contrast, £1 invested in the Family Business Index would have grown to £11.11 – outperformance of nearly 30 per cent by these family public companies. Across the complete 21-year period of the study, compound growth in the Family Business Index totalled some 12.15 per cent, as opposed to 10.85 per cent for the All Share.

The research results, confirming that on an extended timescale family companies outperform the market as a whole, replicate the findings of an earlier US study that showed even greater outperformance. The Pitcairn Financial Management Group of Philadelphia analysed the share prices of 165 US listed companies with a minimum of 10 per cent family ownership, that had been in existence from 1969 to 1989.[3]

Their results indicated that a US$100 investment in 1969 in the basket of family businesses had risen to $2700 by 1989, equivalent to a compound growth rate of almost 18 per cent per annum. This compared with $1 invested in the Standard &

---

[3]*Barron's* (11th February, 1991 issue) carried a detailed analysis of the Pitcairn study.

Poor's 500 Index in 1969, which would have been worth $700 in 1989, equivalent to a compound growth of only 10.2 per cent per annum. The Pitcairn basket of family companies outperformed the S&P Index every year except 1974.

The disadvantages

As well as immensely valuable advantages, family businesses are prone to some serious and endemic disadvantages (summarised in Table 1.3). In the same way that family business strengths are not unique to family firms, neither are their weaknesses, but family businesses are particularly vulnerable to these failings. Many of the problems hinge on the inherent conflicts that can arise between family and business values, and this crucial area is looked at in much more detail later in the chapter.

Rigidity

Walking through the doors of some family businesses can be like entering a time tunnel. Sentiments such as, 'Things are done this way because Dad did them this way' and 'You can't teach an old dog new tricks', reflect the ways in which behaviour patterns can become ingrained and family businesses become tradition-bound and unwilling to change.

Numerous examples came to light in researching this book. For example, the son of the founder of a chain of menswear shops

Table 1.3 *The pitfalls for family businesses*

• Rigidity
• Business challenges
— Modernising outdated skills
— Managing transitions
— Raising capital
• Succession
• Emotional issues
• Leadership and legitimacy

had been brought up in the business and, under his father's direction, had learnt all aspects of its operations. However, he had also learnt that to please his father he should continue to do things in the same way as his father had. Thus, when the son came to manage the firm, he preserved the status quo. The expectations of customers changed, the company did not respond, and eventually it failed.

It is all too easy to find ourselves doing the same thing, in the same way, for too long, and in a family business it is easier still: change not only carries with it the usual disruption and an array of commercial risks, but it can also involve overturning philosophies and upsetting practices established by relatives.

Business challenges

The business challenges which particularly affect family firms can be divided into three categories: modernising outdated skills; managing transitions; and raising capital.

Very often the skills possessed by a family business are a product of history and, as a result of developments in technology or a change in the market-place, these skills can quickly become obsolete. Problems in this area are not necessarily triggered by drastic changes such as the effect of word-processing technology on typewriter manufacturers. They can also arise from subtle changes of emphasis in product manufacture or marketing which can be just as damaging if they catch an unresponsive, tradition-conscious family business off balance.

Managing transitions represents another major challenge for family businesses – it can often be the make or break for a family firm – and, in Chapter 7, some approaches to the issues it raises will be examined in detail. In summary, the challenge to the business is typified by a situation in many companies where the founder is getting on in years and his son, the heir apparent, is convinced that things need to be done differently. The merest hint of this potential conflict can be disruptive, causing enormous uncertainty among staff, suppliers and customers. In many cases the damage becomes even more serious when the son actually begins introducing his programme of radical change. So managing transitions is a difficult challenge to the business and, because of the added dimension of possible intra-family conflict, it is a bigger challenge for a family business than it is for others.

In comparison to the wide range of funding alternatives open to publicly held companies with a diversified shareholder base, family businesses obviously have much more limited options when it comes to raising capital. But over and above this, family businesses commonly have a problem with the very concept of raising money from outside sources.

This tends to occur most frequently in relation to longer-term capital for significant projects, like opening a new plant or creating a new division of the business, but it also shows itself in a reluctance to go to outsiders for bank overdrafts or other short-term funding that would help the firm through quite minor cash flow shortfalls. If funding from the family's own resources means skimping on important projects or inefficiently struggling on through short-term crises then the healthy development and even the survival of the business can be threatened.

Behind these over-cautious attitudes to external finance one usually finds fears about loss of control – fears that will turn up in a variety of guises and contexts throughout this book. The fear can take the form of a mild aversion to outsiders acquiring influence over how the business is run but, more often, deep-seated and intense paranoia is the description that most readily springs to mind. On a day-to-day basis families tend not to want to be answerable to anybody for how they run their businesses, and the idea of the family ceasing to control at least 50.1 per cent of the share capital is usually unthinkable. Loss of control and ceasing to be masters of their own destiny is anathema to most family business people: they feel that control is inextricably linked with the love of freedom and independence that has often been the principal driving force behind the establishment of the business and its subsequent success.

Succession

The passage of a family business from one generation to the next and the change of leadership it involves is a process that is usually fraught with difficulty.

If you change the MD of any company, as well as the obvious managerial considerations, you raise a set of emotional issues that have to be settled at the same time. For example, where there is a defined management hierarchy, decisions have to be made about people's competence to take on new responsibilities after promotion, and what their reaction will be if an outsider is brought in to take on the top job. Again, this is a situation where, on the face of it, the family business faces identical problems to those of other firms, but underlying their problems is a minefield of psychological, family-related, emotionally charged dilemmas which, in reality, entirely transform the change of leadership issue into one that can threaten the survival of the business.

Selecting a successor can often mean choosing between sons or daughters who, until now, have all been harbouring their own secret ambitions of succeeding when their father retires; and the father himself is often ambivalent about succession because he is worried about the ability of his children and how he is to approach favouring one at the expense of the others. But, more fundamentally as far as the business is concerned, almost always the change is not simply a move from one generation to the next – it is a revolution in which the culture of the organisation is reconstructed by the young people who bring with them new ideas about how the business should be run, how it is to develop, new loyalties, new staff, and so on.

So succession represents a major transition, with the fortunes of the firm resting on how successfully it is negotiated. The issue is discussed later, especially in Chapters 7 and 8 which examine succession options, explain the importance of preparation and planning for succession, and provide guidelines on ensuring that the change is accomplished as smoothly as possible.

Emotional issues

The hazards of succession lead on to, and are an aspect of the next pitfall which family businesses have to face up to – the emotional issues that limit the firm's scope for commercial action. This will be discussed in a broader context and in more detail shortly, but here is a good place to introduce the important idea that family and business are two quite distinct domains.

The family domain is emotion-based, emphasising care and loyalty, while the business domain is task-based, with emphasis on performance and results. The family business is a fusion of these two powerful institutions and although it provides the potential for superior performance, it is not surprising that it can also lead to serious difficulties. These can mean patterns of emotional behaviour emerging within the business which, in a commercial context, are deeply irrational and inappropriate: the marketing director does not trust his brother, the finance director, because he used to steal his toys in the nursery – as an illustration perhaps a little bit over the top, but nevertheless indicative of the sort of emotional undercurrents which can be at work; and, not infrequently, the root of the trouble can lie many years in the past – 'Your side of the family swindled our side out of its shares in 1937.'

Leadership
One last drawback of family businesses which is worth highlighting in this initial discussion concerns leadership, or rather the lack of it, in situations where no one within the organisation is empowered to take charge. This becomes especially critical when the business has reached the second generation, and even more so when it reaches the third.

In the second generation scenario, for example, the board of directors may comprise three brothers, all of whom have inherited equal shareholdings, and none of whom has been empowered to take ultimate control – no one has the last word. It is a common weakness among family businesses that there is great reluctance to allocate power. The situation has already been discussed of a father unwilling to plan for succession and to choose which of his children he wants to do which jobs when he bows out. To a large degree, the predicament which our three brothers find themselves in may therefore be their father's fault but, for them, it is too late to dwell on this. It is the responsibility of each generation to resolve its own conflicts so that it is able to empower and legitimise the next generation, and the brothers must define where power lies between themselves before they can even start to think about where it should lie in the future. If they do not, the arrival of the third generation with its increased cast of characters may well herald catastrophe.

In Chapter 4, the typical life cycle of the family business is examined from a predominantly business perspective. However, because the family generation themes already touched on form so much of the backdrop for what follows, it is worth developing them a little now, to the extent that they relate to the formation and growth stages of the business.

FAMILY BUSINESS LIFE CYCLES

A strong desire to safeguard and perpetuate the family business is a primary motivating force for many of those who lead family firms. The reasoning behind this will be different for different families, but some of the most important considerations include:

1. Keeping the business in family hands from one generation to the next is seen as the most effective way of protecting the family's wealth and long-term security.
2. There may be concerns that without the business, family bonds and the closeness of the family unit may be weakened as individual members go their own way.
3. The company is seen as the guardian of family values so that safeguarding the existence of the business becomes a way of preserving strong family values and traditions.
4. Disposal of the business may risk the livelihoods of key employees who have worked loyally for the company for many years.
5. The business may be seen as a monument to the founder or the family – an enduring commemoration of all the hard work and achievement that it represents, and something to be passed on to and preserved by succeeding generations.

So the survival of the business between generations is often a more powerful factor than the one-off financial gain that could be acquired by selling it. At the same time, this transition between generations is a process which involves the most significant changes that occur in the relationship of the family to the business, with each generation facing its own distinct set of challenges that threaten their goal of perpetuating the business.

First to second generation
The family business tends to become more complex with the passing of time, and especially with the transition from one generation to the next. With succeeding generations, the

intensity of emotional factors that surround the family's involvement in the business increases. The 'emotional baggage' – unresolved issues left over from the previous generation – loom ever larger. If, for example, one brother feels he has been 'done down' by another brother, and this grudge is not sorted out before the brothers die, when the next generation succeeds the grievance will live on and fester. The brothers' children will remember it and it will colour their behaviour, leading to emotion-based responses that disrupt the efficient operation of the business.

At the start, however, things could not be simpler – there is an entrepreneur with a dream. Typically, the founder will have left a well-paid job, giving up comfort and security in exchange for risk and a lot of very hard work. Alternatively, they may be taking advantage of an opportunity provided by redundancy or some other type of career break to branch out on their own. Although at an early stage in many business start-ups wives become involved helping husbands (and, increasingly often, vice versa), essentially entrepreneurs are alone at the beginning, relying on their intuition, capacity for work, business ability and total commitment (often at the expense of the family) in order to achieve the first major objective – to see the business become safely established.

Assuming the firm gets through this early survival phase, the nature of the challenge changes. Qualified people have to be brought in, systems need to be set up, and some detailed planning introduced to ensure the firm's development and growth. It is at this time that the founder can find himself personally tested: although there is no question that he remains in charge, the company is beginning to acquire an identity of its own.

The founder needs to develop a new range of management skills which will take the business through to its next level of potential growth. The size of the company means that it now needs a formal structure; individuals with management, not just functional skills must be recruited; decision-making authority must be delegated to senior managers; controls must be put in place to monitor the implementation of decisions. And while all this is going on, the founder's children are growing up.

In order to perpetuate the family firm the founder will usually be counting on his children to come into the business. If this is not what they want to do then outsiders must be brought in to run the firm, and the best ways of approaching this decision are discussed in Chapters 6 and 7. For present purposes, however, let's assume that the children are keen to 'enlist'. Their joining brings a whole new set of problems. For example:

1. What role are they expected to play?
2. What will they be paid?
3. How will their employment affect loyal, non-family employees?
4. How will their performance be evaluated?
5. Do they have sufficient business ability to take over the business?
6. How should a future leader be selected from among them?
7. Who should inherit the shares in the business?

All these questions are made infinitely more complicated by the founder's dual role as parent and employer, as well as by his own, probably ambivalent attitudes about relinquishing control and starting to come to terms with the realities of his age and mortality. For the first time, succession has become a major issue.

A common thread which links almost all the crucial decisions which need to be taken at this time to ensure the successful transition of the business from first to second generation, is that they are decisions which both the founder and his children would prefer to avoid. Of course, there are some owners who intuitively understand the main ingredients of successful transition (discussed in depth in later chapters), such as a unified family, communication, planning and initiating the succession process early, training, and so on. Planning early for inheritance tax is also important (see Chapter 10). Too often, however, the key questions are not addressed, increasing unrest among the founder's children is suppressed, and considerations about the long-term control and direction of the company are lost in the welter of day-to-day business problems.

Discouraged by thoughts of the anguish involved in getting to grips with the really important issues, an almost mystical belief tends to develop – a belief held by the founder, his children, and non-family employees alike – that everything will sort itself out in the end. This rarely happens, and a great many firms are unable to survive the process of succession from one MD to another, a fact demonstrated by research showing that about 70 per cent of firms have a life expectancy of around 24 years – the average tenure of an owner/founder. So failure to plan for and guide the succession process through to completion in the founder's lifetime usually means family trauma, a bonanza for the inheritance tax division of the Revenue Commissioners and, most probably, it will signal the end of the family business that the founder has laboured so long and hard to establish.

Second to third generation
The transition from second to third generation is often easier for the family to cope with. They will already have successfully come through the cross-over from first to second generation, almost certainly learning a lot from the experience.

In addition, members of the second generation have a number of factors working in their favour: the business they have inherited is up and running; the founder has probably ensured that they received a better education than he did; they may well be more skilful when it comes to business management; and they may represent a source of fresh enthusiasm and vigour that can take the business into a new phase of expansion and growth. Some successors, on the other hand, having grown up in a protected atmosphere of comfort and financial security, may not share their parent's dedication to the family business. They may have joined under a feeling of obligation, and their lack of motivation and commitment can lead to the firm's demise, often accompanied by a deterioration in family relationships.

Second generation members face particular problems in relation to ownership of the business. Whereas the founder probably enjoyed both total control and 100 per cent ownership, his successors find themselves operating with a new leader, who they may or may not whole-heartedly support, and as co-owners, perhaps even with only a minority stake. And when they come to consider succession, they must face a similar type of problem to that with which the founder had to grapple, but on a much larger scale. There will usually be more succession candidates when the second generation comes to decide which of their children should take over the business (a situation often exacerbated by equal second generation voting power and a history of unresolved conflicts); also, cousin relationships will have become an issue. Cousins will have, as one of their parents, an in-law who grew up outside the family, and he or she may hold radically different values as a result. This diversity means that in the transition from the second to the third generation, an important challenge involves developing effective communication, leadership and conflict-resolution skills among cousins.

The third generation and beyond
By the time the third generation is in place, there is a well-established business, and there may be several dozen family members who have some sort of stake in it.

As already mentioned, an important characteristic of the third generation is its diversity. A range of in-laws is likely to have become involved as brothers and sisters have married people with widely differing values and perspectives, and they themselves have had children. The diversity can be such that is difficult to believe that all the children come from the same family, and some will grow up loving the family business because they were taught to by their parents, while others will hate it because they feel trapped in it. At this stage it becomes vital to have some sort of escape mechanism in place before the inevitable conflicts arise – a mechanism which provides internal liquidity so that shares can be bought and sold – enabling those who want to exit from the family business to do so. The grim statistic that only 14 per cent of family businesses survive through the third generation is a clear reminder of the importance of such mechanisms, and they are examined in detail in Chapter 9.

Strategic issues in the transition from the third to the fourth generation, over and above those which affect every generation, frequently centre on a loss of direction and purpose. The drive, ambitions and objectives of the founder may all have become no more than an interesting piece of family history, or the original goals may have been overtaken by events in a changing world. Family members often feel hemmed in by a conflict between a desire to be rid of an historical relic which they are now perpetuating from loyalty rather than choice, and not daring to dispose of the business for fear that they will be cast as the traitor who sold out 80 years of family tradition.

At this point, either the company is actually sold or the vision must be recreated by members of the third and fourth generations revitalising the business by engaging the family's enthusiasm and commitment to its future.

The case history on the fifth generation shoe manufacturer and retailer, C&J Clark (see following Chapter 3), highlights many of the points in this section. The firm had around 1000 family shareholders with no direct management involvement in the business. When things are going well, such a *'rentier* class' is generally happy to sit back and watch the dividend cheques flow through the letterbox. But if the income stream dries up, it can provoke a revolt so painful that the independent existence of the business may soon come under threat. As happened at Clark's, those running the business can find themselves in serious peril in the face of angry family owners suffering an income cut and having no proper escape route to allow them to sell their shares: surprisingly quickly, pride in the family inheritance, a stable family business culture and so on can turn sour, and the pressures on everyone to end the feuding and sell up may prove very hard to resist. Selling a business should be precisely timed in order to secure the best price and, needless to say, a sale in the above circumstances almost by definition represents the worst possible timing.

FAMILY AND BUSINESS: CULTURE, VALUES AND OBJECTIVES

In many ways the family business is just like any other in that it aims to create wealth by producing goods or providing services: to achieve this it employs people who all have different backgrounds, abilities and personal goals, but who combine to pursue the organisation's objectives of operating as efficiently as possible to generate revenue and profits. In one key respect, however, the family business is unique: its directors, managers and employees share a family relationship, the ethics and behaviour patterns of which are, to a greater or lesser extent, carried over into the workplace. The final section of this chapter is devoted to looking at the effects that this family relationship can have on the business – on how it is organised and how it operates – and particularly the inherent conflicts that exist between the emotional factors that govern family life, and the objective nature of business management.

Family systems and business systems

A helpful framework for looking at the relationship between the family and the business is to think of the family as a system and the business as a system. In doing this, the initial concern is not with the characteristics of individuals within the two systems, but rather the features that tend to define the relationships between individuals in each system. The emphasis of these features within the two types of system is distinctly different, as illustrated in Table 1.4.

The family system is emotion-based with its members bound together by deep emotional ties that can be both positive and negative. These ties, and indeed a great deal of behaviour in family relationships, are influenced by the subconscious (the need for brothers to dominate brothers, fathers to be stronger than their sons, and so forth). The family system also tends to

Table 1.4 *Family and business: a systems' perspective*

Family system	Business system
Emotion-based	Task-based
Subconscious behaviour	Conscious behaviour
Inward-looking	Outward-looking
Minimising change	Exploiting change

be inward-looking, placing high values on long-term loyalty, care and the nurturing of family members. In addition, it is a conservative structure operating to minimise change – keeping the equilibrium of the family intact.

The business system, on the other hand, is based on the accomplishment of tasks. It is built around contractual relationships in which people do agreed jobs in return for agreed remuneration and, for the most part, behaviour is consciously determined. It is also oriented outwards towards producing goods or services for its market-place, while emphasising performance and results – i.e. the competency and productivity of its members. To help ensure its survival, the business system operates to make the most of change, not to minimise it.

In the non-family business these two basically incompatible systems operate independently, but in the family business they not only overlap, they are actually interdependent. Their differing purposes and priorities produce the special tensions which exist in family firms, creating at the point of overlap (Figure 1.1) operational friction and value conflicts for the founder and other family members.

Family first or business first

Concentrating on family involvement as a source of weakness in firms should not be allowed to obscure the many advantages attaching to the family relationship, discussed earlier in this

Figure 1.1 *Overlapping systems*

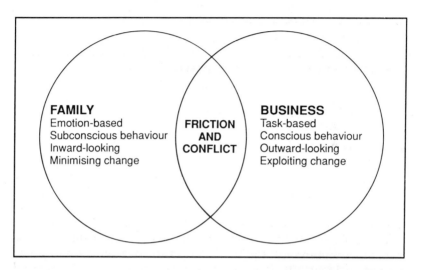

chapter. Here, however, the concern is to highlight the negative impact of an undue transfer either of family values to the business or business values to the family.

Family values in the business
The answers to questions such as how to evaluate the business performance of family members, how to transfer power, and whether and how to share ownership of the business can be very different depending on whether you are looking at things from a family perspective or a business perspective – in short, from a standpoint of family first or business first. Here are some common examples of family first solutions:

1. Adult children are expected to join the family business and commit their working lives to it regardless of their aptitude, abilities or inclination.
2. Nepotism can lead to a management system that favours family politics at the expense of everything

else. This may put the company at a competitive disadvantage by burdening it (right up to the MD level) with incompetent family members and by demotivating able non-family managers.

3. Some families dictate that all family members must be paid equally, regardless of their abilities and how much they contribute. Others pay family members more than they are worth or, alternatively, less than they are worth on the basis that they have an obligation to contribute to the family enterprise and money should be the least of their concerns.

4. Childhood sibling rivalry can develop into serious business in-fighting and become a destructive force that threatens the family firm's survival. This is discussed further in Chapter 3.

5. The family tenet that children must be treated equally is often reflected in owners leaving their children equal shares in the business, regardless of their contribution.

The effect of business on the family

The incursion of the business system into family life can be just as damaging as the reverse situation.

Building a business often becomes an obsessive preoccupation for the owner, and his single-mindedness can undermine the quality of family life. Similarly, although at a later development stage when other family members have joined, families can find that they are never free from the business because its influence has come to invade all aspects of their lives. A particularly important golden rule, for example, is no business talk at the dinner table. Yet a surprising number of cases of serious family unhappiness and conflict arise where children and other family members who are not involved in the family firm have come to feel marginalised and isolated as every evening meal turns into a sort of board meeting at which the day's family business successes and problems top the agenda.

If there are business conflicts the problems become many

times more serious. With some families, differences over business policies become so intense, and there is so much proximity both inside and outside business hours, that normal family life simply becomes impossible.

A balanced approach

Conflict arising from the overlap of family and business systems cannot be avoided entirely. However, successful families devise strategies that help them to keep the overlap under control, and to minimise the possibility of the sort of major problems that arise when one set of values engulfs the other.

Attempting to separate family and business life completely is the first response of many people when they begin to see the danger signals. But as well as denying the reality of family and human behaviour, this strategy jeopardises the sources of commercial strength which flow from the family relationship – loyalty, commitment, sharing in a common enterprise, flexibility, and so on. A much more effective approach lies in developing strategies which assist in recognising and analysing family and business issues, and then addressing them in a direct way to ensure the correct degree of balance between system components. The 'correct degree of balance' is one which allows the business to be run properly while not disrupting family harmony, and the main steps that can be taken to achieve this objective involve professionalising the business, preventive maintenance, distributing power and resources thoughtfully, and managing transitions (especially succession) effectively.

Professionalising the business

The key to professionalising is strategic management – covering planning, organising, staffing, directing and controlling. The process extends beyond basic management theory, however, to recognise the critical importance of properly motivated, well-informed, talented people within an organisation which has thought through its goals and introduced systems for monitoring performance in relation to a strategic plan.

Professionalising the business in this way is the ideal first step towards being able to manage the overlap of family and business systems. It focuses attention on a number of human resource areas which are particularly problematic for the family business, such as recruitment, performance appraisal and remuneration. In addition, it begins to strip out many of the emotional factors that obscure and confuse a proper apprec iation of how the business is really operating and, as a result, helps to provide a much clearer analysis of the best way to position the family company for future success.

Preventive maintenance

The aim here is to do something about the huge range of problems that can afflict family businesses before they take hold. Potential areas of difficulty include family concerns, personal dilemmas, management issues and succession, and within these broad categories the number and scope of individual problems is often bewilderingly large.

Two approaches that can be particularly useful in helping families to anticipate and avoid these problems are the development of a written constitution for the family business, reflecting both family and business values, and the holding of regular family retreats and communication sessions. Both these ideas are examined in Chapter 3.

Power and resources

The most important long-term decisions in a family business concern power and resources. Who has, or should have power within the business and control its resources today? What can be done to ensure these resources are managed effectively and without conflict? And how can power and resources be transferred to the next generation in a way that safeguards the future of the business? Too often, the potential consequences of these critical decisions are not understood by the founder or controlling shareholders. They involve a range of highly complex, often interrelated factors, and require structured and very careful consideration.

Transition management

As well as managing the normal business and industry life-cycle transitions, there are three other transitions that are particularly relevant to family businesses, successful handling of which may be critical for survival. They are:

1. *The founder's transition*: the personal development of the founder to assume the different roles and responsibilities demanded at various stages in the history of the business.
2. *The firm's transition*: the move from the simple, product-driven structure of its early days through to organisational maturity, accomplished by professionalising the business as discussed earlier in this section.
3. *The family's transition*: the complex problems of management succession between one generation and the next.

The four principal steps outlined here – professionalising the business, preventive maintenance, careful distribution of power and resources, and effective transition management – all require planning, and much of the remainder of this book is devoted to detailed discussion of each of them, together with practical guidelines and suggested approaches that those involved in family businesses can adopt to help them get the right balance between the family and business systems. First, however, it is important to understand a little more about who these people 'involved in family businesses' actually are – their differing perspectives, concerns and objectives – and this is the subject matter of Chapter 2.

2 The Cast of Characters

Family businesses are unique because of the people who are involved in them. These people are not just a random cross-section of employees, managers, directors, advisers and investors – they are family members and they are all related to one another. Sometimes, particularly in the early stages, the family involvement is confined to just two or three individuals. But one characteristic of families is that they tend to expand, and successful family businesses generally follow suit, becoming, at the same time, ever more complex organisations.

Whatever the size of the business, each family member has his or her own set of attitudes, opinions, objectives and problems. As a result, an important aspect of understanding how family businesses operate involves an awareness of the background and the unique perspective of each of the major participants.

FOUNDERS

Arising from his extensive research on family businesses, Dr. Peter Davis of Wharton Business School has drawn a helpful distinction between entrepreneurs and founders:

> Though all founders of family businesses are entrepreneurs, not all entrepreneurs become founders. Founders are typically intuitive and emotional people. They obviously

have the drive and ambition to build a great business, but they also have a feeling about the place, a love of what they have created that makes them want to perpetuate it through the generations.[1]

He goes on to identify three types of founder, calling them proprietors, conductors and technicians. Because the attitudes and behaviour of founders are particularly relevant as they approach retirement, this type of classification will be discussed in some detail in relation to succession management in Chapter 7. Their personalities colour all stages of the development of family businesses, however, and in many cases their influence even persists long after they are dead. So before going on to examine business owners as entrepreneurs, as well as the other characters who feature in the family business drama, it is useful to introduce the main characteristics of founders (summarised in Table 2.1) that Peter Davis has highlighted.

Proprietors
For proprietors, ownership of the business (as opposed to mere control of it) is central. Their identity tends to be completely wrapped up with that of the company, they have little trust in anyone's ability to make decisions apart from their own, and they dominate their children and other members of the family involved in the business in the same way that they dominate everyone else.

The children (especially sons) are expected to enter the business as a matter of loyalty, but the founder (most often the founder/father) wants simply to control them, not to develop their talents with a view to ensuring a smooth succession. They may become dependent and submissive in the face of the founder's behaviour, seeking out a quiet existence in some part of the organisation which involves as little contact with their

---

[1]Davis, P. (1990). 'Three types of founders – and their dark sides'. *Family Business*, February.

Table 2.1 *Family business founder types*

Proprietors
— Ownership is key
— 'I am the company – the company is me'
— Business never professionalised
— Children are controlled and become passive or rebellious

Conductors
— Control is key
— Central to most decisions but good at delegating
— Encourage and orchestrate children's involvement
— Proud of family and family business
— Avoid decisions which could threaten paternal role, especially about succession

Technicians
— Build businesses based on technical or creative skills
— Dislike management details
— Delegate administration to key non-family managers
— Children sometimes encouraged, sometimes not
— Conflict between children and non-family managers
— Find it difficult to let go or to pass on skills

---

father as possible: they often find a niche as the firm's resident computer expert – because their father does not understand how to switch a computer on. Alternatively, they adopt a rebellious strategy. The classic result of the latter course is a turbulent saga of resistance and fighting back against the founder's authoritarian regime, and a steadily deteriorating relationship that often ends with the son buying out the father as they both take their own separate ways.

Another aspect of a founder wanting to dominate the organisation to the extent that others are excluded from any real power or responsibility, is that family businesses under the control of proprietors are hardly ever professionalised. Professionalising involves, as a minimum, strategic management of planning, directing, controlling and staffing, and it places emphasis on the importance of properly motivated, talented people within an organisation. This type of cool-headed, rational analysis based on trust and delegation of responsibility is anathema to most founders in the proprietor category.

Proprietors tend to be the legendary characters of family business, perhaps the most famous example being Henry Ford and his dictatorial control of the Ford Motor Company. In the first 30 years of this century, he built the company into the most successful industrial enterprise the world had ever seen, but then, during 15 years of paranoia and obsessive behaviour, he reduced it to virtual bankruptcy. Edsel, his only son, became president, but throughout his tenure Henry Ford remained alive and wielded the real power in the company. Edsel was admired for his creativity, his consensus approach to management and for his good judgement, but his presidency was purely nominal. All his important ideas were blocked by his father, who belittled him in public. He became a pawn in a huge and destructive power struggle, eventually emerging from the process a broken man.

Conductors

Like proprietors, conductors are also firmly in control, but they are much more willing to build up a good staff, delegate responsibility and actively foster efficiency and harmony in the organisation.

Conductors like the idea of a family business, and they like the idea of their children joining the company and working with them. Thus, they invite and orchestrate the involvement of the children and, to preserve harmony, often encourage them to take over different areas of the operation – so one may assume responsibility for marketing, another production, and a third financial administration.

Conductors are proud of the family and of the family business. They work to engender a sense of common endeavour, loyalty and family warmth within the company, and you will often find their offices full of family photographs. But our portrait of warm amiability should not obscure the fact that conductors are firmly in control, and much of their behaviour is directed to bolstering their own paternal role and ensuring that they are the ones conducting and organising the firm's development. As the business matures, the conductor avoids facing the dilemma of succession and having to favour one of his children at the expense of the others. Tensions begin to build up below the surface, but a business culture has been created that is not well equipped to take stress, and the fabric of both the business and family relationships is put at risk.

Technicians

Davis's third category of family business founder is the technician. They build companies based around their creative or technical skills and are often very obsessive types, at home in drawing offices working on wonderful designs and products which only they fully understand. But they generally dislike administration and the day-to-day details of management. Thus, unlike the conductors, they are not orchestrating and usually will have brought in non-family managers to whom they delegate the organisational role in the business.

Although technicians are happy to give up control over administrative details, they are usually not very concerned to pass on their special knowledge to their children who do not possess the same technical skills. Their knowledge and skill is like a magical sword, an Excalibur endowing them with the prestige and power they want. The last thing they want to do is to give it away, especially to their children, who might eventually usurp their position.[2] The children thus tend to move into administrative positions in which they will not be competing with the founder (nor receiving much respect from him for their efforts) and, as a result, often find themselves in conflict with entrenched non-family managers.

---

[2]Ibid.

Despite finding it difficult to let go, and a reluctance to turn over the business to his children, the technician, as he gets older, often discovers he has little room for manoeuvre because he may be so vital to the success of the business it is worth little to outsiders without his presence. In the end, what usually forces him round is the realisation that unless his technical skills, which are at the core of the business, are passed on, the company he has built will not survive.

Most family business founders fall into one of the three categories described here but, as with all such attempts to pigeonhole human personality, it is important to emphasise that the groupings, although helpful, are to an extent arbitrary in that many founders will exhibit some characteristics of all three.

Having looked at examples of types of founder (all of whom are entrepreneurs, although not necessarily vice versa), to understand the complicated dynamics of family businesses it is important also to examine owners from a slightly different perspective. They may not all be planning to found a corporate dynasty but, nevertheless, they do share a number of illuminating characteristics.

THE MALE OWNER

While the owner of the family business may be capable in business matters he often has no formal management training and, as leader of the business as well as patriarch of the family, the owner has to try to balance heavy, and frequently conflicting responsibilities. The pressures can be enormous, with the preservation of the business and the harmony and financial security of the owner's family riding on his ability to succeed.

Many family business owners have something in common: they are entrepreneurs who, psychologists tell us, tend to be alike in many ways (see Table 2.2). They are often difficult, highly individualistic people who have the instinctive conviction that only they are right, combined with the confidence and willingness to take on the responsibility of finding out.

Table 2.2 *Entrepreneurial characteristics: some examples*

• Difficulty in addressing issues of dominance and submission
• Structure experienced as stifling
• Acute fear of helplessness: avoids being at mercy of others
• Low tolerance of independent thinking
• Fear of being victimised
• Looking for confirmation of suspicions
• Secrecy
• Need for applause

The need to achieve personal goals is central to their characters, and personal satisfaction (i.e. building a successful business) is usually a stronger motivating force than financial reward. Frequently charismatic, they tend to be very creative and innovative, not in any theoretical, contemplative sense but in a highly action-oriented way. Thus, they usually have more ideas than they can realistically cope with in any given period, and are weighing up their next plan before they have stopped thinking about the current one. At the same time, they have extraordinary physical energy and stamina and an apparent capacity for almost constant activity.

As well as these attributes that are, for the most part, ideally suited to enterprise building, the owner often has more than his fair share of less attractive characteristics. He is often dictatorial and domineering in both his business dealings and his family life. In the business this tends to discourage the development of all but the most determined and capable subordinates, which, at first, may not matter. The owner's management style is generally instinctive, and unlikely to involve much formality or planning. Such an approach may work well as long as the business remains small enough to continue as a one-man show. But as it grows, shortcomings in the management process – target-setting, planning, organising and controlling – at first become limiting and then become dangerous. All too often the owner unwittingly guarantees the demise of his business by failing to build into it a collective purpose that can ensure its survival after he is no longer around to pull all the strings. For owners who are keen to keep the business in the family, the major challenges are to recognise, prepare and install successors, and to provide for the new ownership of the enterprise in the next generation.

The owner's wife

Starting up and running a new business can become an all-consuming passion for everyone who is closely involved with the owner. Traditionally, although the owner's wife accepted the tendency of the business to invade almost all aspects of domestic life, she usually knew little about it and was content with her role of supporting her husband in his endeavours while staying at home and bringing up the children.

In today's environment, we tend to recoil instinctively from this description which is so completely at odds with the modern viewpoint of women in society. This reaction is understandable, but there is reason to believe that being married to an entrepreneur at least partially insulates women from liberating social trends. No doubt such women have rather more room for independent activity and personal ambition than would have been the case 40 years ago. But the evidence suggests that, for the most part, entrepreneurs' wives come to accept that in order to get along they must become totally supportive of their husbands' work and ambitions. In the last analysis, they know that nothing will stop their husbands doing what they have set their hearts on.

Wives who are able to accept this state of affairs often become important stabilising influences in their husbands' turbulent lives. They can play a number of subtle, behind-the-scenes roles as confidante and business adviser, including acting as sounding board for their husbands, often on issues of character and human perception and, more prominently, as family leader and a symbol of unity, fostering teamwork and communication. As wives and mothers, their first priority is the preservation of the family, and often, when there is conflict in the business between the father and the children, the owner's wife is the mediator who prevents a family civil war.

It is very important, both from a family and a business perspective, for the owner to talk regularly to his wife about how the business is developing, his problems and his plans for the future. Even if she is working in the business this is often as an employee rather than as a partner. Sharing will provide the wife with the feeling she has some control over her destiny, that she is more able to support and encourage her husband and, at the same time, will ensure that she is better prepared in the event that one day she may be forced to take on his responsibilities.

What if there's a second wife?

A family business owner's remarriage may follow on from the death of his first wife or, much more likely, from marriage breakdown. An increasing percentage of first marriages in Ireland end in separation, and for couples where one or both partners are involved in running a family business the percentage is almost certainly higher. It is not surprising that the business-related stress reported by owners, together with worries over financial uncertainty, working too many hours in the week and having too little time for family and friends, often puts an impossible strain on marriages.

As well as marrying into the family, the newcomer is marrying into the family business, whether she will actually work in it or not. She risks having to counter suspicion and isolation as well as the range of problems (business overlapping with personal life, and so on) faced by every owner's wife. As regards the children of an earlier marriage, the newcomer will often be younger than their mother and possibly not much older than themselves, and such factors frequently trigger resentment. At a more tangible level, the appearance of a stepmother can pose a real obstacle to the position of children in the business, and to inheritance.

Owners in this situation can do a lot to prevent or alleviate the problems arising from marriage breakdown by thinking through the range of personal as well as business-related ramifications, and discussing the situation candidly with their existing and new families. Non-family directors can also help by providing an objective viewpoint.

THE FEMALE OWNER

More women in Ireland than ever before are now business owners. During the 1980s, the rising trend in female ownership was the main highlight of new business development, principally in the sole-trader sector, but also among partnerships and limited companies.

Women tend to start businesses for the same reasons as men – self-satisfaction or freedom and independence are much more important motives than profit. It seems that a lot of the fulfilment for women owners springs from their desire to advance beyond the limitations they have encountered as employees in sectors of corporate life that continue to be male-dominated.

The available evidence suggests that female business owners are generally more creative and assertive than their male counterparts. They have usually had to work harder to reach a position of authority – for example, some bank managers still prefer to lend money for new businesses to men rather than to women – and they drive a much harder bargain once they have reached that position. It has also been noted, however, that female entrepreneurs are apt to have even more difficulty than men in learning to delegate responsibility; there is often a stronger desire to oversee all operations and to maintain a much tighter control over the business.

The need for family support is just as critical for women entrepreneurs as it is for men and, if they have children, this can become even more important. Anita Roddick had two children aged three and five when she started the Body Shop in 1976, and she received enormous help from her mother who looked after the children during the day. The Body Shop example also highlights the fact that because women's lives (and needs) are different from men's, they can often be sensitive to opportunities that men may have missed. Roddick responded to the need for change in the elitist cosmetics industry by providing less expensive products in more convenient quantities, using natural ingredients in refillable and ecologically friendly packaging.

HUSBAND AND WIFE TEAMS

Husbands and wives in business together is not a new phenomenon, but what is new is a greater degree of business equality between the partners. Whereas, traditionally, husbands have been the entrepreneurs while their wives may have played vital but behind-the-scenes roles in family firms, couples are now taking steps to ensure that the wife is recognised as a full and equal partner.

As with so many other aspects of family businesses, there are few hard-and-fast rules. For some couples, being together all the time can be a recipe for marriage breakdown; for others, shared business experiences, like shared personal experiences, can strengthen and enrich their marriage. What does seem clear is that while complementary temperaments and talents are particularly important, in addition, the couple must be able to work together as a team. This means that they have to decide how they are to share the workload, allocate power and divide up the rewards of their efforts.

Especially difficult problems arise in relation to decision making and role definition. Some husband and wife teams find that making joint business decisions can be the key to success, while others divide decision-making responsibilities either according to agreed strengths and weaknesses or with reference to previously agreed roles, so that the partner with authority in a certain area makes all the decisions in that area. Clear role definition is crucial, as is conscious separation of business and family issues so that criticisms or conflicts about business decisions do not become personal.

Sharon Nelton, who has conducted extensive interviews with married couples in business, has drawn together some of the common themes in successful husband and wife teams.[3] The main factors include:

1. marriage and children come first;
2. the partners have enormous respect for each other;
3. there is a high degree of close communication;
4. their talents and attitudes are complementary;
5. they define their individual responsibilities carefully;
6. they compete with the outside world, not each other; and
7. they keep their egos in check.

At the end of the day, couples planning to go into business together should realise that they are entering a potentially disastrous emotional minefield. It has to be a step they both fervently want to take, but even then it may be best to include an outsider (possibly a non-executive director) in the company structure from the start – someone who will be able to offer a balancing viewpoint (or even a casting vote if conflict arises), defuse tension, and help the couple to avoid the slippery slope to rivalry, jealousy and blame. If marriage breakdown should ensue, the split-up will usually apply to the business as well.

SONS

Although daughters are becoming more prominent in family businesses, the most common relationship still revolves around fathers and sons. Many fathers and sons get on very well with each other both at home and at the office. Indeed, when the relationship works, it is difficult to imagine a business team that functions more effectively. But this situation represents the exception rather than the rule, and psychologists tell us that father–son relationships have a unique potential for conflict –

---

[3]Nelton, S. (1986). *In love and in business*. New York: John Wiley & Sons. Reprinted by permission of the author. All rights reserved.

"WHOEVER REFUSED TO ADDRESS MY BOY AS 'SIR' HAD BETTER APOLOGISE!"

they represent an area in which the friction between family culture and business culture, discussed in Chapter 1, is brought most sharply into focus. As such, rivalry between father and son can spill over from the family into the business, often with destructive, even catastrophic results. Because of their importance, father–son relationships will be examined in detail in the next chapter.

DAUGHTERS

With the advancement of women in business, daughters are increasingly being considered as candidates for positions of power in family firms, and for succession.

Throughout human history, sons have been favoured in the rules and customs that govern family hierarchy and succession by the younger generation. As the pendulum swings towards more equal treatment of daughters, much more thought is now being given to the special qualities and skills that they can bring to the family business scene. It should not be concluded, however, that equality has arrived – it seems that daughters are still likely to be preferred only in situations where there are no sons, or when the daughter is the eldest child.

The second-class treatment of women generally in the corporate world has traditionally been justified on the basis of doubts about their long-term commitment. It is difficult to decide if views like this represent a cause of such treatment or a rationalisation of it after the event, but what does seem plausible is that, for fathers, it may involve questions of family as well as business loyalty, with daughters perceived as likely to marry and thereby switching their allegiance to another man and his family.

Very little is yet known about how the growing numbers of women in family firms may further complicate family–business relationships. It is interesting, however, that the favourable contrast of father–daughter relationships with the difficult father–son equivalent is cited by many owners of family businesses in which a daughter's rise to power has come as something of a revelation. Fathers seem more able to accept advice about the business and some criticism from daughters, and they often say that they would react to sons saying the same thing as if it was a personal attack. Psychologists suggest that the answer probably lies in a combination of two factors. First, fathers tend not to see daughters as any sort of threat and, as a result, are more willing to consider what they say in a rational way. Secondly, daughters are brought up to be more nurturing, more attuned to emotional needs, and more concerned to give priority to family harmony. As such, their primary business motivation is, and is seen to be, a desire to help their fathers and the family as opposed to a single-minded pursuit of corporate or career development.

This does not mean that daughters are weaker or less effective as far as their role in the family business is concerned. They tend to be emotionally committed to the business and, not infrequently, extremely determined and ambitious individuals. By the time a daughter joins the firm, she will have typically proved herself in other companies or settings, and the odds are that she will have had to train harder and work harder in order to achieve her position.

IN-LAWS

Marrying someone whose parents own a business has some clear benefits, but also a range of potentially serious difficulties that need to be managed carefully. On the benefit side, the family is likely to be wealthy, close-knit and exceptionally strong, and in-laws may often have opportunities to work in the business and even eventually to share in its ownership.

The principal problems relate both to the in-laws' new family and the business, and include:

1. Feeling like an outsider. Even when the spouse does not work in the family business, he or she is likely to be involved in endless discussions and meetings about it and the new in-law tends to feel excluded.
2. Feeling overwhelmed by the spouse's family. Business families share a common, often all-encompassing passion about the family firm, and they tend to be forceful and extremely energetic. Newcomers, with no prior experience of such families may find them bewildering and may also feel under intense pressure to conform to the family norms.
3. Being treated with suspicion. New in-laws, whether sons or daughters, are frequently seen as a threat to the status quo – their arrival on the scene forces the family to examine how they are likely to fit in and whether they should eventually have any claim to ownership in the business; areas, as has been seen, that many business families prefer not to anticipate, plan for, or even think about.

Coping with these types of problem, at least initially, should be based on a straightforward, common-sense approach. It is important, for example, to avoid establishing a relationship with the family and the business exclusively through your spouse – develop family friendships quietly and sensitively to encourage acceptance and trust. Never take sides in family conflicts and do not try to act as a family therapist – however good your intentions, they will inevitably be misunderstood. Aside, however, from a general strategy incorporating preparation, patience and calm diplomacy, special problems arise for sons and daughters-in-law, especially in relation to the decision whether to join the family business, and these may require a different type of approach.

Many families put pressure not only on their children, but also on their children's spouses to work in the family firm. Their contribution may prove to be a disaster or a tremendous success – usually there is no half-way house here, and the outcome tends to be at one of these extremes. There is the traditional stereotype of the ne'er-do-well son-in-law who has married the boss's daughter for the financial rewards of working in the business. Despite an absence of suitable motivation, and probably also competence, a job is found because of who he is not what he is, and the results tend to be predictably calamitous for all concerned. Alternatively, he may be a committed family member, highly motivated to making a worthwhile contribution to the development of the business, and talented enough to succeed.

One factor contributing to this polarisation between very bad or very good is that in-laws working in the business usually find themselves in a situation in which, almost regardless of their performance, family members treat them as outsiders, and non-family employees believe they have got the job solely because they have married into the family. They thus find that their deficiencies swiftly become the focus of attention, and if they are to be accepted they must prove themselves to be very good indeed. To help overcome both types of opposition it is a valuable idea for new in-laws to acquire outside experience before they join the family firm. With their contribution under the spotlight, there is no substitute for competence.

Some male owners find that they are able to enjoy a better relationship with their son-in-law than their son, because of the absence of father–son conflict. Others are not willing to risk the consequences of discovering whether this is true for them and, like the Rothschild family, impose an inviolable rule that sons-in-law are not permitted to work in the business. An alternative, although just as dogmatic approach to the question of in-laws, is for business families, as a policy, to insist that all family members contemplating marriage enter into a pre-nuptial agreement with their spouse stipulating that specified assets – principally shares in the business – remain the property of those who owned them before the marriage. The device, which enjoyed some popularity in the United States in the early-1980s, is designed to avoid any part of the family enterprise falling into the hands of the new in-law. It is now generally viewed with distaste, however, on the grounds that families attempting to demand such an agreement are acting oppressively, and that for the young couple involved it represents a violation of trust that is liable to create long-term bitterness.

MULTI-FAMILY OWNERSHIP AND PARTNERS

The majority of family businesses consist of a single family unit involving parents and children. As if this structure is not complex enough, the problems multiply exponentially when more than one family unit becomes involved. This is generally what happens if the business survives through to the second and third generations.

Consider the case, for example, where an owner bequeaths the business to his two children. If they each have two children who inherit their parents' shares then the single owner in the first generation is replaced by two in the second and four in the third and, while the second generation comprises siblings, the third consists of both siblings and cousins. If the business is started by unrelated partners the problem of proliferating ownership can become more acute, more quickly. If two partners bequeath their shares to their respective families, there are likely to be five or six shareholders in the second generation and twelve or fifteen in the third.

Because it poses such a dilemma for a great many family businesses, sibling rivalry will be looked at in detail in Chapter 3, where it will be seen that the best solution revolves around agreeing strictly defined roles and responsibilities for siblings in family firms. It is worth mentioning here, however, that some experts believe siblings, despite jealousy and rivalry, actually have a better chance of forming a working business relationship than people who have not grown up together. By the time they are in business together, brothers and sisters, even if they do not necessarily love and trust each other, do know how the other thinks, how they respond to pressure, what motivates them, and they will usually have developed conflict-resolution skills. Cousins have no such historical bonds – they originate from different families and may hold different values. Indeed, because they are the co-product of in-laws from outside 'the family', their values may be radically different.

Multi-family ownership requires such a unique combination of people, skills and attitudes, it is not surprising that so few family businesses survive beyond the third generation. Rules must be developed which strictly define and regulate family involvement in management so that efforts to develop a strong, professional organisation are not undermined by family domination of managerial jobs.

Others will have decided that the wholesale transfer of management to outside professionals is the only answer, although leadership may still come from key family members. However, if voting control is spread around the family, there is still the risk of the differing needs of family members causing disagreement or out-and-out warfare (as, for example, happened recently at C&J Clark, the fifth generation footwear manufacturer and retailer – see the case history following Chapter 3). In practice, the best way to avoid chaos in these circumstances is through some form of centralised share ownership, particularly voting trusts.

NON-FAMILY EMPLOYEES

This chapter on the family business cast of characters would not be complete without some discussion of the under-researched role of non-family employees.

Successful non-family employees in family businesses are often interesting characters with a distinctive psychological make-up that helps them to fit into an unusually demanding working environment. The job does not suit everybody, and there are many instances of talented managers who have resigned because they have run out of opportunities, or because the politics and emotional cross-currents in family-owned companies have become too much of an interference in their work. But managers who are able to cope with such factors are often very good indeed.

At one company visited during the preparation of this book, the MD had been trained by his father's most senior manager. The training was hard and, in the style of the company's founder, rather autocratic. The senior manager has now retired but still visits the office once a week to chat to the MD and, to make himself useful, does a little filing. This type of loyalty is difficult to imagine outside a family concern.

Sometimes, however, key employees are not willing to stay on unless they are given financial incentives, including shares or share options. Surrounded by an atmosphere of family friction, and working with family members who may have acquired their positions as a result of favour rather than competence, there is a tendency for non-family managers to feel that they are the only people doing any real work and they ought to have a stake in the success, despite adversity, of their efforts. As share ownership is generally kept in the family, this often results in an impasse. One possibility is for the company to issue non-voting shares to the employee, or shares with restricted transferability. Alternatively, 'phantom share options' can be created – they do not involve real shares at all, but they do enable the employee to participate in any future appreciation in the value of the company. (These devices, along with other incentive plans, are examined in detail in Chapter 5.)

In fact, most employees in family businesses do not expect to own shares in it. They often enjoy the informality of working in a closely knit team, as well as the personal relationship with the boss that may be unobtainable in large, public companies. Employees derive a feeling of confidence knowing they are not simply part of a faceless institution. They are happy as long as they are reasonably well paid, treated with respect and given the opportunity to fulfil their career aspirations. However, employees often have concerns about family involvement. The autocratic management style of an owner can inhibit the development of competent managers, or make it difficult to keep them. Many who are competent worry about the effect of family tensions on the business and on their ability to get on with their job properly. At worst they fear becoming pawns in a family power struggle. They are also frequently unsure of their job security in circumstances where the owner is not planning management succession, his children are probably not qualified to run the business, and the most likely outcome is that the company will have to be sold.

Another source of insecurity arises from the fact that family members may be suspicious about the loyalty of non-family employees who, as a result, find themselves excluded from key planning or operational information: unlike family members who 'can't leave', the freedom of employees to do so, taking specialist knowledge with them, becomes a major worry for some owners.

On occasions, the role of a loyal trusted employee within the organisation is cleverly institutionalised by the family. A respected senior manager can thus become a counsellor and mentor to the next generation and, if the owner dies before one of his children is ready to succeed, may even be asked to run the company for a temporary period. Reliance can also come to be placed on non-family managers for more structural reasons. As a family business matures, particularly by the time it reaches the third generation, it tends to acquire its own identity, distinct from that of the founder. At the same time, management by consensus will have become a problem because there are so many family members, all of whom have a stake in the business. This combination of factors often leads to greater dependence on non-family managers as the best means of maintaining the continuity of the business.

The subject of non-family employees, particularly their role in the management of family businesses, will be discussed further in Chapter 5.

3 The Family's Approach to the Business

The quality of family relationships is crucial to the success of the family firm. Sometimes the business itself is a unifying force that brings the family closer together. Too often, however, an entrepreneur starts a new business that flourishes beyond his wildest dreams, but rather than adding to the quality of family life it serves as a catalyst in its destruction. Emotional tensions surface between family members that split the family and destroy the business.

The previous chapter included a review of the various possible factional divisions within families that can interfere with the effective functioning of the family business, impeding communication, frustrating adequate planning and preventing rational decision making. Here the objective is to highlight the two types of family conflict that can most seriously disrupt the operation of the business – those deriving from the relationship between fathers and sons and from sibling rivalry. Such sources of conflict can never be entirely eradicated, but gaining an understanding of the nature of the psychological factors which underlie them is a vital step in being able to limit their destructive consequences.

Next, the characteristics shared by strong families are examined to see what it is that enables them to resolve many types of conflict successfully, as well as to reduce the number of insoluble conflicts to a minimum. An attempt is made to draw together the lessons of all this, explaining how families can develop a cohesive approach to the business by agreeing on a family strategic plan.

THE MOST SERIOUS CAUSES OF CONFLICT

In Chapter 1, the family and the business were analysed as two distinct, essentially incompatible systems. Family behaviour is emotion-based and powerfully influenced by the subconscious, whereas the business system revolves around accomplishing tasks and generally entails behaviour that is consciously determined. When family emotional issues and subconscious needs (frequently expressed in the form of aggressive and/or destructive behaviour) turn up and are played out in the context of the family business, their impact can be devastating.

This impact need not take the form of an outburst of suppressed emotions that suddenly makes it impossible for family members to continue working together (although there are famous instances of such spectacular débâcles). More often, family-based conflict in the business finds expression in constant bickering, with the process of arguing usually much more important than the subject matter of disagreements. Battles are fought out time and time again, over the same ground – a war of attrition that can carry on for years, draining the company of its strength, vitality and, eventually, its life-blood. The two most serious causes of such internecine strife are hostility between fathers and sons and sibling rivalry.

Father–son relationships

Unlike father–daughter relationships which tend to be relatively trouble-free, the complex relationship between fathers and sons has been the subject of considerable study by psychologists and family therapists, and a general review of the current state of knowledge on the subject would be both impractical and inappropriate in this text. What follows, therefore, represents a summary of the most important research conclusions, related as closely as possible to those aspects of father–son relationships that especially influence not only the emotional health of the parties but also the welfare of the family business.[1]

It is worth emphasising that father–son relationships are not always bad news. There are many fathers and sons who love and respect each other, and who find that working closely together, far from causing tension, is the most natural and easy thing in the world. Indeed, their relationship is often a source of unique strength and, as a result, they are able to form an effective and formidable business partnership. Unfortunately, however, such fruitful teamwork is relatively uncommon, and it is important here to examine why problems arise.

A helpful approach involves looking at the relationship between fathers and sons from the point of view of the psychological needs of each, and a good starting point is the father's perspective as founder of the family business. It has already been noted that many entrepreneurs see the business they have created as an extension of themselves – a device or instrument that represents, above all else, their source of personal fulfilment, gratification and even masculinity, as well as the symbol of their achievement. The people that work with the founder and for him are characteristically his tools in the process of shaping the organisation that will become his monument when he dies. Consequently, he guards power jealously, finding great difficulty in delegating authority. Consciously, he may want to facilitate his son's entry into the business, planning gradually to transfer responsibility to him and, in due course, to pass control of the business on to him. Subconsciously, however, he needs to be stronger than his son: he feels that to yield the business to him would be to lose his

---

[1]In this section we acknowledge especially the work of the distinguished business administration authority Harry Levinson and, in particular, his paper: 'Conflicts that plague family businesses.' *Harvard Business Review*, March–April 1971, 90–98. Copyright © 1971 by the President and Fellows of Harvard College; all rights reserved.

masculinity, and that if he lets his son 'win' he will be removed from his centre of power. These contradictory influences often lead the father to behave in erratic and inexplicable ways, sometimes appearing as if his sole motivation is the welfare and development of the business, and at others as if he is hell-bent on its destruction.

Turning to the son's perspective, he develops his own feelings of rivalry that are a reflection of his father's. Psychologists tell us that rebellion against parental authority is a natural phase of a child's development, and when the parent is also the employer and source of economic sustenance for an adult child, this phase may be repressed. In addition, as he gets older the son needs and seeks increasing independence, responsibility and executive power in the organisation, but finds that he is denied it by his father who refuses to cede authority. Often the son, desperately eager to take on running the business, is left on the sidelines for years – way beyond the age when others of comparable ability and experience in non-family businesses would expect to take over. The father, not infrequently, refuses to retire despite repeated promises that this is what he wants to do, and the son's frustration is made many times worse by this type of contradictory signal. The discrepancy between what the father says and what, by his actions, he apparently really means becomes evermore irritating. Levinson illustrates the dilemma well:

> The father often communicates to the sons that he is building the business for them, that it is going to be theirs, and that they should not be demanding of either appropriate salary or appropriate power because they are going to get it all anyway in due time. Nor should they leave the father and the business because it is self-evident that he has been good to them and is going to give them so much. Thus they are manipulated into an ambivalent position of wanting to become their own persons with mature, adult independence on the one hand, and the wish to take of what they are being offered on the other. If they leave, seemingly

they will be ungrateful. If they threaten to depose the father or demand to share his power, then they will indeed destroy him. If they don't do as he says, then they are disloyal and unappreciative sons.[2]

So we have a situation characterised by mounting tension as the father looks on the son as ungrateful, potentially even treacherous, while the son sees himself the victim of emotional blackmail and feels both hostile to his father and guilty for his hostility.

As Levinson explains, within the family business these conflicts manifest themselves in many different ways. The father often actively cultivates an atmosphere of ambiguity which allows him to 'call the shots' as events occur, rather than being bound by clearly defined rules; the son wants and needs clear direction. Similarly, the father is generally most comfortable deferring decision making until the last possible moment; the son wants decisiveness. These behaviour patterns foreshadow the types of problem the son is likely to face when, and if, he eventually does take over. Often the father has retained obsolete management principles and techniques, or the company may have grown beyond the capacity of one man (i.e. a man other than the founder) to control it effectively. The son finds himself faced with the task of repairing an organisation full of previously concealed weaknesses, and the job may well prove too much for him, with the company joining the ranks of family businesses that cannot survive (or at least survive independently) beyond the tenure of their founders.

Some strategies for trying to cope with the psychological elements that underlie father–son relationships will be examined shortly. First, however, it is necessary to look at another

---

[2]Levinson, H. (1983). 'Consulting with family business: What to look for, what to look out for.' *Organizational Dynamics*, Summer, 74–82. Reprinted by permission of the publisher, © 1983, American Management Association, New York. All rights reserved.

major source of family conflict that jeopardises the efficient functioning of family businesses.

Sibling rivalry

In the middle of this gloomy catalogue of conflict, it is perhaps worth pausing for a moment to redress the balance by highlighting a success story emphasising that not all family businesses are beset by crippling intra-family struggles. Sherry Bros. Limited is a substantial manufacturer of furniture under the 'Rossmore' brand. The business was established over 30 years ago by two brothers, later joined by a third. Over this period they have expanded a business that originally employed 5 people to one employing 85 – from one which originally made cheap furniture for the home market to one that now makes quality furniture and exports 50 per cent of its output to the UK.

The three brothers are all quiet, modest men. 'One of the reasons that the business has been so successful is that we three are very close' says Pat, the middle brother and chairman of the board. 'We are all personally committed to our religion, our work, our families, our employees and the community in which we live, and we have found this to be a winning combination'. The brothers live in the vicinity of their factory and have a deep involvement in community affairs.

But it is important to face up to the fact that sibling rivalry, while clearly not a problem for the Sherry's, nevertheless represents a potentially crippling obstacle to the successful development of a great many family businesses, and it is critical that we understand why and how it comes about before looking at some of the ways in which it can be contained and controlled.

Psychologists believe that sibling jealousy is rooted in the deep desire of children for the exclusive love of their parents. Underlying this is the child's concern that if a parent shows love and attention to a sibling, perhaps the sibling is worth more, and the child is worth less.

An older brother, dominant as a child by virtue of age, size and competence, is resented by his siblings. A sister is jealous of her sister's perceived beauty or is forced to be 'the good one' in order to compensate and redress the balance for her sister's bad behaviour.[3]

Sibling rivalry is normal and, in a family context, can be seen as a useful competitive ingredient in relationships that stimulates the healthy development of well-adjusted, coping adults. But there is an assumption in this interpretation that adult siblings will take their separate paths in life, leave the parental home, establish separate families, follow separate occupations, and so on. With family businesses, this normal 'growing apart' of families is inhibited and we have a situation where childhood rivalry between, for example, brothers for their father's affection is perpetuated into adult life as a result of the necessary day-to-day contacts between them arising from their roles within the business. Thus, we find the rivalry exerting an adverse influence on how the business is run, colouring management decisions and, if left uncontrolled, eventually paralysing the organisation.

The custom of favouring elder sons in family hierarchies, especially in relation to inheritance, extends to family businesses where elder brothers are usually marked out to succeed their fathers, thus confirming the younger brother's belief that his elder brother is indeed preferred. At the same time, the elder brother tends to view the younger as less able, leading him to distrust and over-control his 'junior', restricting his freedom and his opportunities to take on responsibility. Younger brothers thus often try to carve out a special position for themselves in the business – exclusive (and independent) responsibility for its administration, for example – in an attempt to compensate for the childhood relationship and to demonstrate their ability and competence to themselves, their brother, and to others.

On occasions, and often without realising they are doing it,

---

[3]Faber, A. & Mazlish, E. (1987). *Siblings without rivalry*. New York: W.W. Norton (and published in the UK in 1988 by Sidgwick & Jackson).

owners intensify sibling rivalry by fostering a competitive spirit among family members in the business – effectively reinforcing and magnifying the rivalry that already exists. More commonly, yet just as problematical, the family tenet of parents treating their children equally will probably have been applied to the family business, with the result that brothers own equal shares in the organisation, both are members of the board, and sibling rivalry is thus 'locked' in place.

WHAT CAN BE DONE ABOUT THESE PROBLEMS?

Only rarely can the difficulties that flow from father–son, sibling and other forms of family rivalry be completely avoided. By their very nature they are facts of life in the vast majority of family businesses and the key issue is whether they are allowed to dictate behaviour and become a destructive force that threatens the survival of the business. In other words, can family members learn to manage the conflicts rather than be managed by them?

On the positive side, business families do tend to have something of a head start when it comes to conflict resolution and conflict management – possession of these skills is generally one of the hallmarks of strong families, and lasting family businesses are usually owned by strong families. Research on family functioning draws relatively unanimous conclusions about the main characteristics that distinguish strong, healthy families from their less capable counterparts. In

Table 3.1 *Characteristics of strong families*

• Commitment
• Appreciation and communication
• Time together
• Spiritual health
• Coping with crises and stress

general terms, 'optimal families' as they are often dubbed, demonstrate those skills that are crucial in dealing with the tensions between individual choice and group needs – between the need for individual freedom and for belonging and togetherness. More specifically, their common qualities, excellently summarised in Stinnett and DeFrain's study, *Secrets of Strong Families*,[4] fall into five categories (set out in Table 3.1).

The first concerns commitment, manifesting itself in the importance that family members place on family unity, sharing the same goals, and concern for each other's welfare. While family members are encouraged to pursue their individual goals, the commitment to family would preclude pursuits that threatened the best interests of the family.

Under the second category, appreciation and communication, we find that members of strong families have the ability to recognise each other's positive qualities and to share open and frequent communication. An important aspect of these qualities is that such families establish very clear boundaries between, and emotional space around members: there is an acceptance of differences and respect for personal choice while working towards shared goals. Thirdly, strong families enjoy time together, not just in quality terms but also as regards the quantity of time; not allowing outside pressures to pull them into going separate ways, yet not stifling individual identities – closeness without coercion. There is usually 'joy in relating', and this can include organising time together at regular family gatherings, family meals, or family attendance at religious services.

Fourthly, strong families share a unifying force that encompasses integrity, honesty, loyalty, and high ethical values – attitudes which may be categorised as 'spiritual health'. Whether this spirituality is expressed in terms of organised

---

[4]Stinnett, N. & DeFrain, J. (1986). *Secrets of strong families.* Boston, Mass.: Little, Brown.

religion or through a moral code, many such families gain strength through a belief in a higher power that can influence their lives.

Finally, strong families are good at coping with crises and stress. They tend to keep problems in perspective and handle them by focusing on the positive elements and by pulling together, seeking outside help when it is needed. Their ability to communicate freely, respect for individual choice, and a strong base of spiritual health are important assets in dealing with crises and in enabling them to resolve conflicts among themselves.

It is worth emphasising that, of course, the foregoing portrait of the strong family is, at the end of the day, a psychological model. Yes, there are families in which these attitudes are to be found; in which these skills are present; but the description gives an overall impression of near perfection that is, thank goodness, rarely encountered in the real world. Nevertheless, it is not hard to see how valuable many of these qualities are when they are carried over into the family's participation in the business and, as such, they form an excellent backdrop against which to examine some particular strategies for coping with the types of conflict discussed earlier in this chapter.

Conflict prevention and management
First and foremost, it is vital for family members struggling with the debilitating consequences of both father–son and sibling rivalry to appreciate and understand the psychological basis of their dilemma. Without this, there is an inevitable tendency to believe that all the aggression, the destructive and irrational behaviour, and the guilt involved are a result of purely personal or unique family defects. Once it is realised that what is being fought out is a series of primeval rivalries that affect not just individuals but most of the human race, this cannot fail to begin to defuse some of the intensity of the emotions generated by the problems, thus making it easier both to analyse what is going on and to begin thinking more clearly about alternative ways of coping.

Discord between father and son

Unfortunately, experience shows that most entrepreneurial fathers, even when they understand the processes that are at work, are not good at getting to grips with their dilemma themselves. Their fears over losing control and suffering rejection seem to make it difficult for them to grasp that there may be valid alternative points of view which they can accept without appearing to be irresolute and weak. This means that much of the responsibility for taking positive action falls on the son's shoulders.

A father who pressures rather than invites a son to join the family business is sowing the seeds of future conflict, and the son's recognition of why he chose to join is often very important. As Levinson explains:

> Most sons will say that it is because of the opportunity and the feelings of guilt if they had not done so. Often, however, the basic reason is that a powerful father has helped make his son dependent on him, and so his son is reluctant to strike out on his own. He rationalises his reluctance on the basis of opportunity and guilt. Struggling with his own dependency, he is more likely to continue to fight his father in the business because he is still trying to escape his father's control.[5]

A son should also recognise how his own feelings of anger and rivalry naturally lead to defensive measures on the father's part and to increasingly entrenched positions on both sides.

Communication between father and son is crucial. The son should explain that he recognises how important running the business is to his father, and how much of his personality is wrapped up in it, but that it is just as important that he has an independent area of opportunity in which to develop his own

---

[5]Levinson, H. (1971). 'Conflicts that plague family businesses'. *Harvard Business Review*, March–April, 90–98, at p.96.

skills and responsibilities. One possibility is for the son to establish a new venture, either creating a division within the existing company framework or via a new subsidiary, over which he has managerial autonomy. A variation on this might be a corporate restructuring under which the group creates a core operating division to be presided over by the son, while the father controls the remaining activities and pursues new ventures. Approaches such as these have the advantage of providing the son with space to grow and mature while, at the same time, avoiding the possibility of appearing to desert the father. However, it is important that the father in these circumstances should hive off an economic unit and not a section which is struggling. If this were to happen the results could be disastrous: a son, anxious to prove his ability to his father yet incapable of making profits in a unit which should have been closed down long ago, is really fighting an uphill battle.

Serious cases of father–son conflict may require third-party intervention. The neutral third party – perhaps a business friend or a specialist counsellor – should understand the nature and intricacies of the problems that father and son are grappling with, and should begin by talking at length with both parties privately to build up a picture of the history of their relationship and a clear view of their feelings. Father and son should then discuss the situation together in the presence of the inter-mediary, who must try to ensure that the real issues are debated – the father's fears over losing control, the son's rejection of him, or dependence on him and so on – and that a specific agenda is drawn up of agreed ways in which the parties plan to try to change their behaviour, together with possible organisational changes of the type already mentioned that will reduce the potential for conflict.

If all these measures are unsuccessful, the son is faced with a choice of learning to tolerate the situation until events arise that change it, or leaving the business to seek opportunities elsewhere. In either case, it is not uncommon that the passage of time works to heal divisions between fathers and sons, especially after the son has established his own family and reached a level of maturity at which he no longer sees his parents as omnipotent, but feels a genuine compassion for them as individuals with real needs, fears and dreams.

Rivalry between siblings

Once again, a path needs to be followed that starts with gaining an understanding of the psychological nature of the posture each sibling adopts towards the other, and continues with them talking together about their mutual feelings and behaviour and, if necessary, enlisting third-party help. If possible, however, the siblings themselves should try to prevent their rivalry becoming destructive by acknowledging its harmful potential and agreeing on a code of behaviour that recognises their mutual dependence and puts in place a procedure for resolving disputes, perhaps with the assistance of independent board members.

As well as talking through and thus demystifying their feelings of anger and guilt, siblings need to consider how they can divide their roles in the family business in a way that enables each to demonstrate competence, reduces the potential for competitive conflict, and increases their chances of finding ways of working together in a complementary relationship. If the organisation is large enough, rivalry can be minimised by siblings taking responsibility for separate areas, defined operationally or geographically (or preferably both). The aim is to help them focus on their own jobs and not on those of their siblings. In addition, it helps if remuneration and job titles are defined in advance according to objective criteria. This will tend to reduce the emotional repercussions should one sibling perform better and achieve more than another. Again, independent directors are potentially valuable here because they can help to contribute objectivity to (and remove some of the emotional sting from) important decisions involving siblings, such as promotion and management succession.

Communication

The importance of direct communication between family members in limiting, *inter alia*, conflict in the organisation is

"... I SAID...'I THINK IT'S ABOUT TIME WE UPDATED THE COMMUNICATION SYSTEM!!"

difficult to overstate. The ability to share open and frequent communication has been highlighted as one of the hallmarks of strong, coping families. It was also stated that family businesses are often owned by such healthy families. Unfortunately, however, the truth is that adequate communication is often in short supply in family businesses. The problem was emphasised by Sir John Harvey-Jones in relation to a number of the firms he examined in the *Troubleshooter* series of television programmes, first broadcast in 1990. In his book, based on the series, he says:

> Family businesses, where everyone enjoys working together and where there is a great deal of mutual respect for each individual's contribution ... can suffer from a lack of frankness. It can sometimes happen that the bonds of love

and respect are so strong that individuals are constrained from saying what they really feel, for fear of treading on someone else's cherished aspirations.[6]

Sir John made these comments in the context of discussions with actual families and this may account for the measured and diplomatic flavour of his analysis. The reality is that people in family businesses generally dislike the idea of working through family issues and difficulties – they find it very hard to talk about them, let alone to analyse what is going wrong and what needs to be done to ensure the problems do not interfere with the efficient functioning of the business. There is often a sort of forbidden agenda covering a whole variety of potentially sensitive family issues that might generate unpleasant conflict. Despite the fact that many family conflicts can only be truly resolved if they are tackled early enough, the unspoken understanding is to 'let sleeping dogs lie'.

In addition, the secretive management style of many owners can further inhibit communication. The origins of this desire for secrecy are difficult to unravel: some owners say they feel guilty about accumulating a disproportionate amount of wealth compared to their employees; with others it relates to their excessive need for control which, at least in part, can be maintained by severely rationing information. Yet it is the owner himself that usually suffers most as a result of this secrecy. Rather than sharing family-related business problems with his family and gaining their support in resolving them, he bears the burden alone, while an atmosphere is created that fosters rumour and speculation, and frustrations and tensions build.

The blend of family and business is demanding and complicated in the best of circumstances, and impossible in the

---

[6]Harvey-Jones, J. with Masey A. (1990). *Troubleshooter*. London: BBC Books. Extract reproduced with the permission of BBC Enterprises Limited.

worst. However, if owners, their spouses and their children can learn to communicate and share their thinking with each other about the important issues the family must face up to, and if the children have a forum in which they can express their opinions openly and take part in policy making, it is possible for the family to develop a cohesive approach to the business. In seeking to achieve this aim, establishing organised procedures and a formal framework in which dialogue can take place is enormously helpful.

A FAMILY STRATEGIC PLAN

A family can significantly improve its chances of success by planning its future together, establishing clear policies governing its relationship with the business, and defining the responsibilities of family members.

The process of developing a family strategic plan helps families to approach their businesses in a unified way, rather than as a group of individuals that just happen to be related. The chances of misunderstanding are greatly reduced when the objectives and the rules are clear, and the rules are much more likely to be adhered to if they are arrived at through consensus rather than edict. Open communication not only improves a family's chances of preserving harmony, it also forms a sound foundation for the business strategic plan that will be discussed in Chapter 4.

Strategic planning in a family context consists of:

1. Addressing the critical issues relating to family involvement with the business.
2. Establishing a family council to provide a forum in which family members can discuss their views and concerns, and that allows them to participate in policy making.
3. Developing, in writing, a statement of the family's values and policies – in other words, a family constitution.

4. Monitoring the family's progress and maintaining regular communication through periodic meetings.

Before moving on to look at the detailed planning process, mention was made above of the importance of 'consensus' rather than 'edict' when developing a family strategic plan. Dictionary definitions of 'consensus' tend not to go much further than 'agreement', but the notion is so central to developing and implementing a successful family plan that it is important to try and pin down what 'consensus' really adds up to in practice. As part of his family business research, Dr. Peter Davis of Wharton Business School also became interested in this concept, and decided to ask leaders of the Quaker religious community in America what consensus – obviously a key tenet for this peace-loving movement – meant to them. Several helpful points emerged from these conversations about the true nature of consensus:

• An understanding of, and unity with, the ideals of the organisation that make consensus rather than majority rule preferable.
• An understanding of the individuals that constitute the group, and their idiosyncrasies.
• A deep commitment to listening.
• A clear sense of trust in the validity (even the divine validity) of each member's contribution.
• An openness to learn from those who may be better informed in an area of particular concern.
• An acceptance of the fact that individual knowledge untempered by group wisdom is very often shallow.
• A willingness to undertake deep self-examination, particularly when a compromise between one's own point of view and that of the group could lead to consensus.

The planning process
The stages involved in developing a clear and concise family plan are illustrated in Figure 3.1. As with any strategic planning

Figure 3.1 *Developing a family plan*

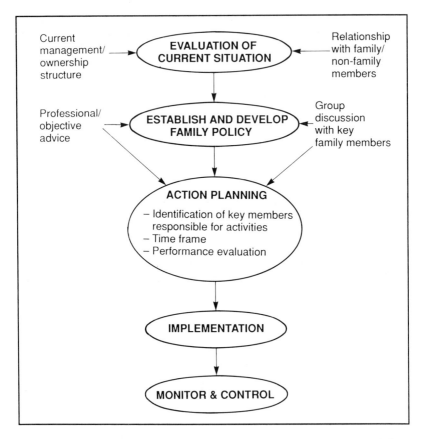

exercise, the first step is to evaluate the current situation. This will involve looking at the state of both the business and the family, including factors such as the current management and ownership structures, the family's relationship with the company, and the role of non-family employees.

In stage two, the family develops its policies and objectives, starting with its long-term goals for the business – for example, is it to remain a family company, or is the family looking to sell up or go public in five years' time? In the light of this, policies should be defined covering the critical area of family–business relationships, such as the involvement of family members in the business, share ownership, and management succession – a list of the factors that are likely to merit consideration at this stage of the planning process is set out in Table 3.2.[7] An experienced family business consultant can often help families to decide on their goals and policies by bringing an objective perspective to this critical stage of the planning process. The involvement of a professional outsider may also be valuable when the family meets to discuss the issues raised by its strategic plan, and the role such a facilitator can play at family meetings or retreats is examined later in the chapter.

Defining policies is followed by action planning. This will include identification of family members responsible for implementing particular aspects of the plan (who is to organise family council meetings, who will mediate in cases of conflict between family members, and so on), setting a timetable for implementing the plan, and deciding how its implementation is to be monitored, controlled and evaluated.

A family council
The establishment of a family council provides an organised forum for family members to participate in the development of their strategic plan and in future policy making. They have a chance (perhaps for the first time) to start tackling the 'forbidden agenda' and to lay down some clear, sensible ground rules governing their ownership of, and involvement in, the family business. Even if all family members do not agree on every question, they at least have a voice in the process, and in many ways it is the setting up of this process that is the key step

---

[7]Adapted from a summary in Benson B., Crego, E.T., & Drucker, R.H. (1990). *Your family business: A success guide for growth and survival*. Homewood, Illinois: Dow-Jones Irwin Inc.

Table 3.2 *Checklist for developing a successful family plan*

Long-term goals
— What are the family's objectives for the business?
— Keep it in the family?
— Sell it eventually?
— Go public?

Management philosophy
— The best interests of the family should be paramount?
— The best interests of the business?
— A combination of the two – and if so what?

Family members in the business
— What should be the criteria for entry?
— Should in-laws be allowed to join?
— How will the roles of family members be determined?
— How should family members be remunerated?
— How should their performance be evaluated?
— What if family members do not perform up to appropriate standards?

Share ownership
— Should shareholders regard themselves as owners of an asset that will yield them a capital sum in due course, or simply as custodians of the shares (which are perhaps placed in trust) for the next generation?
— If the shares are viewed as a realisable capital investment, is everyone aware of this and are procedures in place to accommodate holders who want to cash in their shares?
— Alternatively, if the shares are seen as a non-transferable trust for future generations, is everyone aware of this and is the company geared up to provide income and pension rights in place of capital asset status for the shares?
— Who will be allowed to own shares in the company?
— Who should have voting control?
— What should the dividend policy be?
— What will happen as regards share ownership in the next generation?

Table 3.2 (contd.)

— Should family members who are active in the business be treated differently from those who are inactive?

Management succession
— What should be the criteria for selecting the next leader?
— When will the transition take place?
— What should be done if the choice is wrong?
— What are the owner's aspirations in retirement?
— How can the family help the owner to achieve them?

Relationships within the family
— What responsibilities do family members have towards each other?
— What is the best way to ensure an atmosphere that enhances mutual respect and support?
— How should intra-family differences be dealt with?

Other matters
— Should the business have independent directors?
— If so, how should the family relate to them?
— How can the family protect the security of loyal employees?
— What role should the business have in the community?

– as well as providing a structured opportunity for the family to assess and organise its relationship to the business, it puts needed pressure on individual family members to face up to the difficult emotional issues that, uncontrolled, can be so damaging to the business.

As regards the composition of the family council, some prefer to limit inclusion to family members who are active in the business. However, unless there are persuasive reasons to the contrary, the council is most effective when both 'passive' and active family members (and their spouses) are included. All family members, whether directly or indirectly, have a stake in the business and it is best if everyone is fully involved from the start – the objective, after all, is to establish a unified and cohesive *family* approach to the business.

Retreats

An excellent way to begin a family council is with a one-day retreat, with relatives gathering in a quiet environment away from the everyday surroundings of job and home.[8] A non-confrontational atmosphere will help them to discuss their future in a constructive way, and all the main issues in the family strategic plan (summarised in Table 3.2) should be on the agenda, perhaps with the aim of setting out the conclusions of the discussion in a draft of the family's constitution (see below).

The chances of a successful retreat are greatly improved by inviting an impartial person from outside the business and the immediate family to act as a facilitator. Ideally, this should be a professional consultant who is experienced in helping family-owned businesses, and he or she should be responsible for setting the agenda, chairing the meeting, and ensuring an atmosphere in which everyone feels free to express their concerns.

To help identify the issues, the facilitator will usually interview the company's principals in advance of the meeting, and draw up questionnaires to be completed by all the participants. This will help to ensure that discussion at the meeting is tailored to the particular difficulties and needs of the family and their company – the facilitator is not there to solve the family's problems, but to guide the family as it makes its decisions.

---

[8]It's worth emphasising here that the word 'retreat' is used in this sense of a peaceful sanctuary, rather than to mean that the family has been defeated by all the trials and tribulations of family business life and is in full-scale retreat. In a recent case, the lady MD of a family company, alarmed by these possible negative connotations, insisted that all the documentation for the family's day be rewritten so that 'the family retreat' would read 'the family advance'!

The family constitution

It is a good idea for families to record the conclusions of their strategic planning in a written family constitution – essentially a statement of intent that spells out the family's values and its policies in relation to the business. Many families, after a day-long retreat, are in a position to put together the first draft of their constitution, which is later ratified by all family members at a future family council meeting.

In the end, of course, it is possible that not all family members agree with every single provision of the constitution, but at least the rules have been thought about, discussed, written down, and are clear, and the family can avoid the turmoil that so easily results from ambiguity. Also, the retreat, discussed earlier, should be the beginning rather than the end of family communication. A timetable should be set for future meetings, to be held at least annually, at which the constitution can be reviewed and, if necessary, amended.

By way of illustration, an example of a constitution adopted by one established family business is given below.

A family constitution

Set out below are certain binding principles and practices which we have discussed openly and in detail and which we agree are in the best interests of harmony in the family and the future success of the business. This constitution has been drawn up in the light of the challenging fact that less than 14 per cent of family businesses in Ireland survive beyond the third generation, and it is adopted with effect from the date hereof.

Management philosophy and objectives

Our major priority will be the best interests of our customers. Our company management will combine the highest ethical and business standards. Sound business principles will take precedence over family issues. Each family member understands and accepts this and undertakes never for any

---

reason to place pressure on the board of directors for dividends, jobs, or benefits in excess of what the board feels is consistent with business objectives.

By following this philosophy we believe the business will continue to grow profitably, to provide an economic return for family members, and to provide a heritage for our children.

Family jobs and remuneration
No member of the family will be offered full-time employment by the company unless he or she has gained a minimum of one year's relevant experience in another unconnected organisation.

Entry into the business will be an opportunity, not a birthright, and higher levels of commitment and performance will be expected from family members than from other employees.

Family members will only be employed in positions for which they have the appropriate attitude and experience, and if their performance consistently fails to meet expectations, they will be requested to leave.

In order to limit the potential for future conflict, it is hereby agreed that no in-laws will be permitted to hold positions in the company.

Family members employed in the business will be remunerated on the same basis as non-family members and will participate in performance appraisal in the same way as non-family members.

Leadership
The next managing director will be selected on the basis of professional competence, and will not necessarily be a family member.

We pledge our support for the chosen individual even if not our personal choice.

We have established that our next managing director should satisfy the following criteria:
— Must have a proven track record of performance;
— Must have leadership qualities, the ability to command respect among employees and family members, and vision for the company's future; and

— Must have solid experience in our area of business operations and be an appropriate ambassador to our customers, the community and the business world.

Voting control and share ownership
Only bloodline family members and their direct bloodline descendants may own shares in the company or vote. Voting control will be vested *only* in family members who are personally active as employees in the business, or in a voting trust. No shares in the company may be sold or transferred by any family member, other than to direct bloodline descendants, without first being offered for sale back to the company at an independently appraised value.

Board of directors
In order to provide objectivity, expertise, experience and guidance, a non-executive director will be retained by the board. Family membership will not be a requirement for board membership. All board members, other than non-executive directors, will be required to hold a management position in the company.

Outside professionals regularly retained to provide services to the company shall not be board members.

Bloodline family members not on the board will be permitted to ask questions or make suggestions for board action to the board, and the board will endeavour to respond to such requests promptly.

The board will have responsibility for resolving any conflict among the family on business issues and the board's decision will be final and binding on all.

Communication
We acknowledge the importance of open communication within the family. At least once a year we will have a meeting of the family council which all family members will be entitled to attend.

We will respect the opinions of other family members, even if we do not agree with them. In the event of disagreements, we commit to constructive resolution that places the best interests of the company and the family over our own preferences.

Our employees
The success of our business would not have been possible without our devoted, loyal and hard-working employees. We are committed to the continuance of an environment that values their contribution, treats them with respect, and provides them with appropriate rewards and benefits.

Amendment of the family constitution
The family constitution will be formally reviewed every five years and may be amended or modified at any time by a majority vote of family bloodline members of 18 years or over.

While we acknowledge that this document is not legally binding, we will support the constitution and encourage our children to do so.

The family's approach to the business: Key suggestions

- Both father–son conflict and sibling rivalry need to be understood before they can be managed.
- Sons acquiring managerial autonomy within some part of the organisation can secure space in which to grow and mature without appearing to desert their father.
- To minimise the scope for rivalry, siblings should try to divide their roles in the family business so that they can focus on their own jobs, not on those of their siblings.
- A family can significantly improve its chances of success by drawing up a family strategic plan that establishes clear ground rules governing its relationship with the business and defining the responsibilities of family members.
- Establishing a family council provides an organised forum for family communication, policy making, planning and the resolution of differences.
- The family's strategic plan should be articulated in a written constitution that sets out the family's values and policies in relation to the business.

Chapters 1 to 3: Some concluding maxims

- The difference is our family pride!
- A plan shows you are serious about change.
- Families need a constitution.
- Communication is the critical difference.
- Respect for consensus keeps the family together.
- Empowered leadership is vital for business success.
- No business talk at dinner!

Case Histories

STABILITY AND CONTINUITY

One of Ireland's most successful businesses was established towards the end of the 19th century by the grandfather of the present chairman. The development of the enterprise provides a fascinating story, and the company is now a thriving national firm in its third generation, happily disproving the cliché 'from clogs to clogs in three generations'. There is no doubt that the founder was familiar with clogs, although in his business career his appearance was both formal and formidable. He was determined to make sure, however, that neither he nor his family would ever have to rely on clogs again.

Tom established and ran a successful toiletries shop in a west of Ireland town. He tutored his son well in the ways of commerce, and was anxious that he would take over and run the store. In due course the son joined, bringing with him a greater vision of how the firm would develop in an emerging Ireland. He expanded the retail store and also established a wholesale operation. Still not content with these achievements, he cast his eyes towards the capital city and bought an outlet in Dublin.

The business was developing at a satisfactory if not an exciting pace, when one of those rare opportunities presented itself. The son became aware of a new product that was about to arrive on the market: his gut feeling convinced him that it would become a leader in its field, and so he made the decision. He set out for the UK and the US in turn (at great expense and on what some might have described as a wild goose chase) and secured the distribution rights in Ireland for a new drug. He could already see a new direction for his business and, returning to Ireland, he explained his vision to the firm's most important manager: with an offer of equity shares, he secured the manager's services for the new firm.

Having established the new operation, he sold off the old business to its managers. The new company, with a superb lead product, was able to attract a range of other excellent merchandise and, thus, the business thrived and expanded spectacularly.

The third generation son (the present chairman) then entered the business and earned his spurs by a lot of hard work and intelligence. He sought to consolidate and build further on the solid foundations provided by the previous generations, although it did not come easy and there were many setbacks.

In addition to consolidating and extending the physical structures of the business – premises, plant and stock – he set about improving that most important and oft neglected aspect – the management structure. The directorate was reorganised so that family involvement would be for the benefit of the business, guaranteeing stability and continuity, but at the same time ensuring that the ambitions of non-family members would not be frustrated.

There is now a two-tiered board structure – one tier occupied by non-executive family members and the second tier by non-family executive directors. Any family member wishing to join the company has to undergo the same rigorous selection procedures as a non-family member, and promotion depends on a candidate's contribution to the firm, reviewed regularly as part of the assessment procedures.

The present chairman presides over a strong, expansion-minded company. He is confident in the advice he receives on issues of principle from his family co-directors, and confident also in the energetic performance of the non-family executive directors. A prosperous business means that the company can afford to keep family members happy with modest but consistent dividends, and non-family executive directors enjoy the opportunity to realise their ambitions and are rewarded fairly for the successes they achieve.

INSTABILITY AND DISCONTINUITY

The footwear manufacturer and retailer, C&J Clark Limited, is one of the UK's oldest, independent, family-owned businesses. Clark's is also a household name in Ireland in both the manufacturing and retailing arenas. For many years Clark's operated successful manufacturing units in Dundalk and Kilkenny and there is hardly an Irish person, male or female, who has not at some stage in their lives worn a pair of Clark's shoes.

From mid-1992 onwards, however, years of private family feuding came to a head. After a further few months of acrimonious debate conducted via press statements, a 'solution' involving selling the company was rejected by only a slim margin (52.5 to 47.5 per cent) at an extraordinary general meeting on 7th May, 1993. A number of important lessons emerge from the recent history of Clark's – a history that began almost 170 years ago.

The company's origins can be traced back to the 1820s when the brothers Cyrus and James Clark began making slippers from sheepskin offcuts at their father's farm in Somerset. The arrival of the sewing machine in the 1860s boosted production and encouraged diversification. But real growth did not take place until after the Second World War, at which point Clark's embarked on a programme of factory building and the acquisition of national and international brands.

The business prospered, especially during the 1950s and 1960s when 'Clark's shoes' entered the language as bywords for well-fitting, comfortable footwear. Although a public flotation was considered at various points in its history, the company remained resolutely private and family owned, under the control of an ever-increasing number of the descendants of Cyrus and James. By 1992, with the fifth generation on the board, around 1000 family members controlled 70 per cent of the equity, with a further 10 per cent in family trusts.

In the late-1980s, Clark's business, like the UK shoe industry as a whole, found itself under mounting pressure from the dramatic increase in cheaper imports. Management consultants McKinsey were called in to report on how the business might shape up to this threat; uncompetitive factories were closed down, but reorganisation costs exacerbated the financial downturn caused by difficult trading conditions. Pre-tax profits tumbled from £41.7 million in the year to January 1990, to £20.4 million in 1992, and £1.7 million in 1993. Declining profitability resulted in drastic dividend cuts, angering many shareholders who had come to rely on the family company for a steady income.

This, however, represented only the later stages of a divisive feud that had been developing across the previous decade among family shareholders, the vast majority of whom have no day-to-day involvement in the company's affairs. As well as dividend income, another festering issue centred on the demand that they be able to cash in their shares.

A procedure was set up whereby shares could be traded once every six months with buyers restricted to other family members but, for the most part, potential sellers greatly outnumbered buyers and the system proved ineffective. The company was therefore forced to embark on the expensive business of borrowing money in order to purchase its own shares and, in 1991–92, it spent almost £40 million buying out disgruntled family shareholders representing some 20 per cent of the capital.

The feud culminated in October 1992 in an attempt by a faction of the Clark family to oust two non-family members from the board (including the chairman, Walter Dickson) at a special shareholders' meeting. The rebels claimed long-running disagreements over corporate strategy and aimed to increase family influence on the board. Against such a troubled background, it was not surprising that potential bidders for the company started to emerge.

As the meeting date approached, money remained at the heart of the battle, but the arguments about family share sales and dividend policy extended into a more general debate about how family members could extract the full value of their shares. Despite acrimonious divisions, a consensus emerged among board members, reflecting at that stage probably the majority shareholder view, that the company should be sold.

In the event, the shareholders' vote was postponed pending the findings of a committee set up to review possible bids for C&J Clark and to determine a target price that could be recommended by the board. After examining three bids, the board announced that it favoured an offer from Berisford International, the agribusiness and property development group, valuing Clark's at £185 million. This announcement signalled the final phase of the battle. Family and non-family members opposed to a sale mounted a skilful campaign and, as mentioned above, shareholders voted narrowly in favour of continued independence at the May 1993 EGM.

With the life-span of the vast majority of family businesses limited to two or three generations at most, private family companies of Clark's vintage are clearly the exception rather than the rule. But the bitter row that almost led to the sale of the company highlights the range of problems such businesses can face, and, rather than commenting here, references to the many lessons to be learned from the case study are made at appropriate points throughout this book.

PART II

THE BUSINESS

4 Professionalising the Business

Frequently the most difficult hurdle that owners face is to adapt their management styles to the demands of a larger, more complex business. If the company is to continue to grow, instinctive management methods must give way to a 'professionalised' approach to the business – an approach based on planning and controlling growth through the use of strategic management techniques. This chapter includes an analysis of the typical evolution of family businesses through to this critically important turning point, how to make sure you see it coming, and how to adjust your management style to meet the new circumstances. A broad overview is provided of organisational concepts, the requirements of organisational change, and the main elements of planning, organising, staffing, directing and controlling.

Among many other advantages, professionalising the business is an important step towards being able to manage potential conflicts between family and business values and goals. The process of analysis tends to de-emotionalise the business – a particularly salient benefit as far as most family companies are concerned.

Family firms go through predictable stages of development and growth, and have to cope with a variety of different types of change. The changing life cycle of its products, fluctuating competitive factors, the personal development of owner-managers, and changing family needs all affect the outcome.

BUSINESS DEVELOPMENT PHASES

It is possible to categorise the development phases of successful businesses in a variety of different ways, depending on the type and complexity of analysis and the particular aspects of the life cycle that one is seeking to highlight. For present purposes, the three broad evolutionary stages illustrated in Table 4.1 provide a useful perspective – i.e. phases in which the organisation is product-driven, process-driven and, finally, planning-driven.

Stage one – product-driven development

In the early days of a family business, the organisational structure is simple. The owner has an idea, identifies a market need, seeks and finds capital, and invents, builds, adapts or buys a product or service to fulfil that need.

This stage is usually characterised by an endearing mixture

Table 4.1 *Three stages of business development*

Stage	Characteristics
Product-driven	A product or service is identified and brought to the market in a profitable manner. A production and management system for delivering the product or service is developed.
Process-driven	Success has been achieved in the basic process, and methods and controls are introduced to increase its effectiveness and efficiency.
Planning-driven	The business matures. Planning is used to formalise continuing activities, to provide a basis for effective management, to pinpoint new opportunities, and to promote the future growth of the business.

of chaos and exhilaration. The founder is using his creative energy to put together and shape an enterprise from nothing, and he and his team will be totally committed and working tirelessly because their short-term goal is survival. Systems and formal planning are non-existent; there is no specialisation – everyone is expected to take on everything; decision making is *ad hoc* and based on improvisation; frequent financial crises have to be resolved because the business is under-capitalised; and amidst all the hustle and disarray there is often a lot of fun and excitement to counterbalance the many frustrations.

The chaos is controllable because the founder is personally on top of everything. All the key decisions which might have an effect on the future of the business are taken by this one individual. Less predictably, fear of failure will usually push the founder into seeking control over almost all tasks at all levels in the business, from negotiating bank overdrafts to opening the post in the mornings (worried that somebody else is likely to lose that all-important letter). During this stage, founders also often feel guilty about putting the security of their family at risk as well as about not spending enough time with them. They will involve family members in order to bring them closer to the business, usually as 'helpers' rather than as part of the management team.

Most entrepreneurs love the excitement and the challenge of this pioneer phase and, given a good idea, a receptive market, and enough capital to deliver the product and pay the bills, many enterprises survive through it, on dynamism and adrenaline, to become established businesses – but what happens then?

Stage two – process-driven development
By the time the second stage of growth begins, the business will generally have achieved commercial stability and financial equilibrium. The small band of loyal customers that helped the company through the early days will have expanded to form a solid base of demand, supplier relationships will have become firmly established, sales and profits growth will have stabilised,

and there will no longer be the week-to-week cash flow crisis to pay the wages and the company's other bills.

The owner remains firmly fixed at the centre of all significant decision making although, without relinquishing any real control, some delegation of non-essential tasks may have been introduced. A few organisational systems and controls may also have been put in place to increase the company's efficiency in carrying out the basic processes established in stage one. This is, however, more to do with refining and improving what the company already has rather than looking to the future, and is unlikely to encompass any serious strategic planning.

As the business continues to grow it becomes more complex. Decisions need to be taken on an ever-increasing variety of topics – should the company diversify, employ extra people, move to larger premises, open an office abroad, seek additional capital, and so on – and all these individual decisions have to make sense for the organisation as a whole. The focus, therefore, tends to shift away from the need for entrepreneurial qualities and towards the need for effective management, with the emphasis on co-ordination rather than control.

This is the critical point at which family businesses often get into trouble. At this time, many of the problematical family issues discussed in earlier chapters will be starting to make their presence felt – the owner's children are likely to have joined the company; conflict between fathers and sons and sibling rivalry may be threatening business efficiency; friction between the family and the business systems is probably increasing; and overlaid on all this we find the company at an organisational crossroads. Vital decisions are required that will determine whether the business will organise for growth and lay the foundations for entering the third phase of planning-based maturity, or whether it will fail to get to grips with the need for change, risking, ultimately, its very survival.

The hurdles facing owners who are approaching this critical transition are looked at in detail later in the chapter (see 'Obstacles to professionalising'). There, strategies will be examined that help them accept the need to adapt the organisation to meet the new and complex problems it faces, to successfully decentralise decision making while ensuring effective co-ordination, and to avoid deteriorating business performance. In the meantime, however, let's complete this discussion of the three-stage model of business development by looking at the final stage of maturity.

Stage three – planning-driven development
After a business is successfully professionalised, it can enter the third stage of planning-driven development. This is a period of integration: people, systems, and processes work *with*, rather than *against*, each other, and a lasting, durable business culture begins to take shape.

This, of course, does not mean that all problems just disappear. But once the owner finds *managing* comes naturally, he will cease to be *managed by* events. The company experiences a cultural readjustment that allows it to initiate and adapt flexibly, encourages peak performance, and offers the potential to achieve new levels of growth and long-term profitability. Neither does professionalisation mean that the business becomes a bureaucracy: the intuitive approach and quick reflexes that made the business successful in the first place are not lost – an orderly environment is provided that helps firms to channel and enhance these strengths.

Some of the other characteristics of the planning-driven development phase are as follows:

1. Having shared responsibility with others, the owner is freer to concentrate his attention on providing leadership and vision.
2. The owner's control is founded on his confidence in others to manage their responsibilities.
3. A definable culture for the business begins to evolve, based around decentralised decision making and a cohesive management structure.
4. Growth is controlled through documented, strategic planning that establishes targets and provides people,

money and facilities at the right time to help achieve these goals.

5. Appropriately rewarded managers are involved in the decision-making process and are held accountable for clearly stated and measurable performance expectations.
6. Communication within the company is open, consistent and clear.
7. Outside advisers play a more active role in helping the company develop.
8. Ideally, the roles of family members in the business have been clearly defined along the lines discussed in earlier chapters. Effective, acceptable processes have been established for dealing with family issues that arise in the business, and the family is able to resolve differences constructively and to reach consensus on key questions, including management succession and equity ownership in the next generation.

ACHIEVING A PROFESSIONALISED APPROACH

There comes a time in the development of every business when the owner reaches a saturation point after which he can no longer do everything himself. He can try, but this will mean that he has ceased to make the most effective use of his time – and an entrepreneur's time is his most valuable asset. If growth is to be sustained, the owner must ensure, first, that he recognises his primary role – namely, establishing vision, direction, and a competent and committed organisation. Secondly, he must devote an increasing proportion of his time to performing this role, leaving others to tackle the more mundane, day-to-day responsibilities that it is not necessary for him be involved in. In short, the organisation must become less centralised and must acquire more sophisticated managerial skills that shift the emphasis from control to co-ordination. To accommodate this change of emphasis, it must develop a more disciplined working environment than that which sufficed in the old days, and the direction of the enterprise must be plotted. The major areas involved in this distinction between what can be called professional, as opposed to entrepreneurial management, are illustrated in Table 4.2, and examining how to establish a professional approach to each of them is our principal concern for the remainder of this chapter.

Obstacles to professionalising

For a few lucky entrepreneurs, professionalising their business by planning for and controlling its growth through the use of strategic management techniques is an intuitive process. They instinctively recognise the crossover point after which the temporarily effective but untidy methods that have seen them through the start-up phase will actually begin to become counter-productive, and that a carefully organised approach is

Table 4.2 *Professional versus entrepreneurial management*

Management functions	Professional management	Entrepreneurial management
Development	Planned management development: identifying requirements; designing programmes	*Ad hoc* development, principally through on-the-job training
Budgeting	Management by standards and variances	Budget not explicit; no follow-up on variances
Innovation	Favouring incremental innovation; willingness to take calculated risks	Favouring major innovations; willingness to take major risks
Leadership	Consultative or participation-based styles	Styles vary from directive-based to *laisser-faire*

Table 4.2 (contd.)

Management functions	Professional management	Entrepreneurial management
Culture	Well defined	Loosely defined and family-oriented
Profit	Profit orientation; profit is an explicit goal	Profit seen as a by-product
Planning	Formal, systematic planning: strategic, operational and contingency planning	Informal, *ad hoc* planning
Organisation	Formal, explicit role descriptions that are exhaustive and mutually exclusive	Informal structure with overlapping and undefined responsibilities
Control	Formal, planned system of organisational control, including explicit objectives, targets, measures, evaluation and rewards	Partial, *ad hoc* control; little use of formal measurement

now necessary to integrate all the parts of the business into a coherent and manageable whole. Their intuition also extends to telling them how this ought to be carried out.

For the less fortunate majority, the need for the transition is generally recognised, but only at the level of a vague awareness that something is about to go wrong, and a feeling that a different approach is now required – but what? Family business owners face some significant obstacles when it comes to professionalising the company. Recruiting outside consultants or professional managers to stimulate the process of organisational development presents special problems in family firms because it is necessary to adapt the process to the needs of specific personalities in senior management and in the family unit. The central personality is generally the founder, and founders who do recruit outsiders are often unable to let them get on with their job independently. The obstacles include:

1. difficulties in delegating responsibility;
2. positions of authority may be reserved for family members;
3. fear of loss of control by the family;
4. lack of an alternative vocation available to the owner; and
5. family loyalty towards employees.

The inability of owners to delegate can stem from a lack of trust in others; becoming simply too attached to the business at the expense of outside interests and other career opportunities; or their need for power that prevents them relinquishing control over decision making.

In one company visited during the research for this book, there was a complete lack of trust in the managers. The owner had to involve himself in all activities with the result that the firm was stranded in a narrow market with low margins and low returns. The lack of reliance on professional managers meant that there were no personnel with experience outside the firm, or knowledge about other firms in the same sector. The owner lacked information about other firms and how they compared to his own.

The idea of a management team, which means that others will have a share in decisions, often seems threatening to the owner's highly valued independence. Also, the haphazard process through which many family businesses have survived to achieve their present size (and the fact that most founders do not have any formal management training), tends to encourage the emergence of an unstructured, 'unbureaucratic' management system – and 'why change a winning formula?'

The trouble is that the factors that bring about the need for greater delegation of responsibility (i.e. the pressure to decentralise control as a result of the growth of the business and the increase in the sheer number of decisions to be made), also make such delegation more difficult. The greater volume of decisions is usually accompanied by an increase in the importance of decisions, thus discouraging delegation.

Another common obstacle in family firms is that positions of authority are reserved for family members. The firm's *raison d'être* is to satisfy the material requirements of the family, and the appointment of outsiders does not support this objective. But the expertise that the family is able to provide may be inadequate. Even if outside managers have been recruited, they may find they cannot function effectively because the firm does not operate like 'a normal company', or because the family

"JUST THINK SON... SOMEDAY, ALL THIS WILL BE YOURS..."

interferes to support trusted, long-standing employees who are considered almost as part of the family. The professional manager may find it extremely difficult to develop his own power base and, even in firms that have made a successful transition to professional management, a family figurehead is still often preferred by the staff and customers.

Unfortunately, there are no quick or easy solutions for owners and their families seeking to overcome these obstacles to professionalising their business. It requires a willingness to change, a strong commitment, and someone in the family who is prepared to lead the process and see it through. Some of the ways families can clarify and define their complex relationship with the business by developing a family strategic plan were looked at in Chapter 3. One objective of such planning is to achieve the appropriate balance between family and business – a balance that inevitably changes over time. The transition to a professionally planned and controlled organisation is a time when the balance must favour the business, and every effort must be made to ensure that family issues do not hinder and jeopardise the process, and the firm's future growth.

Professionalising the business and planning are not luxuries – they are essentials. If an owner who has difficulty delegating, and is working harder and harder just to keep pace, can grasp this fact and come to recognise that planning uses time to make more effective use of time, he will soon discover that both the business and his quality of life will benefit. Running a business should be rewarding, creative and enjoyable, not a route to an early grave.

STRATEGIC MANAGEMENT

To reach the planning-driven phase in our three-stage model, the family business must professionalise, and the key to professionalisation is strategic management. The essence of strategic management is to examine and analyse the principal components of the business and to develop plans that reflect achievable goals. The result is the integration of all parts of the organisation – operating systems, structure, strategy, capital, marketing, boardroom and employee resources – into a coherent and manageable whole, with everyone pulling in the same direction. The overriding purpose is to provide a competitive advantage for the business, now and in the future.

It would be out of place in this book to undertake an in-depth discussion of strategic management techniques: many studies examine the subject in the detail it deserves. The object here is to provide an overview of strategic management, with particular reference to the valuable benefits it offers for family businesses, discussing the main components as well as the practicalities of the processes involved. The basic requirements for strategic management are:

1. a strategic business plan;
2. a management plan (implementing the business plan);
3. a capable, properly motivated management team;
4. formal management information and control systems;
5. clear and consistent communication; and
6. outside advice and assistance.

The first step, therefore, is to draw up a strategic plan.

The strategic business plan

The objective of strategic business planning is to provide the company with a coherent approach, in writing, to dealing with the basic management tasks of planning, organising, staffing, directing and controlling (see Figure 4.1). The plan can be seen as a sort of road map to enable the firm to answer three basic questions: Where are we?; Where do we want to go?; and, How do we get there?

The reaction of many owners to these questions is to make clear they left primary school some years ago and to add that such a simplistic approach is unlikely to be of much value to them. But the apparent simplicity of the questions tends to disguise their crucial importance. Owners who take time off to re-examine these fundamentals almost always find that the

Figure 4.1 *Strategic management considerations*

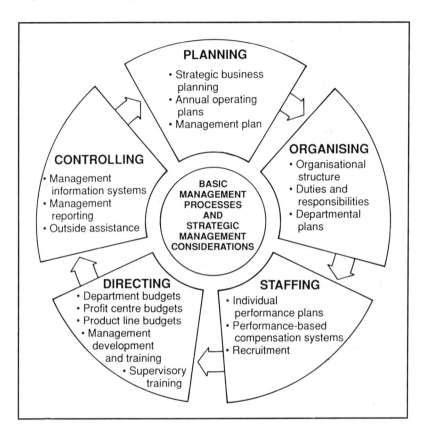

introspective look at their business and the accompanying overview provide a new and fresh perspective on what they are doing, even if they never go on to develop a formal strategic plan. Indeed, thinking about planning and involvement in the planning process, rather than the plan itself, can be seen as the major point of the exercise. Another common objection is that planning is futile because the future is unpredictable. But strategic planning does not attempt to predict the future – it provides a flexible approach to future developments, whatever these may be, so that the company is equipped to cope with the inevitability of change.

The process

The general steps for setting up and implementing the business strategic planning process are:

1. Diagnose the current situation of the business. Decide what are its *internal* strengths and weaknesses (for example, our unit costs are less than the competition but our distribution system is poor), and its *external* opportunities and threats (the European single market may be good news, but the latest technology threatens the usefulness of our product).
2. Develop a business mission statement. A clear definition of the central purpose of the business, its products, services, customers and values.
3. Develop goals. State, in terms which can be measured, the outcomes expected for the business, across the next three to five years, in areas such as growth, profitability and market share.
4. Define strategies. Allowing for contingencies, identify the broad initiatives to be taken and the techniques employed to achieve the specified business goals. Each action point should include the steps to be taken, the people responsible for carrying them out, the time frame, and (see point 5) the resources that will be required.
5. Determine the impact on the business of implementing these strategies. What resources (human, financial, equipment, time) will be required. For example, a financial controller may need to be appointed to take responsibility for running the management accounting system.
6. Write up the plan, incorporating the business mission,

goals, strategies and impact assessment, along with financial and budget projections, into a single document.

7. Implement and monitor the plan. Assess the company's performance relative to the plan at regular (at least annual) intervals.
8. Revise the plan as necessary. Add or remove plan elements to ensure the healthy development of the business. Flexibility is the key to success.

The best approach to developing the plan is to arrange a two or three-day retreat, away from the business, and to employ the services of a facilitator, experienced in strategic business planning, who will act as catalyst, helping to organise and guide the process. (See Chapter 3 for a discussion of retreats and the roles of a facilitator in the context of family strategic plans: the main considerations discussed there are equally applicable to formulating a strategic business plan.) All members of the key management team – owners, family and non-family – should participate. One of the golden rules to remember is that you cannot get people fully supporting a plan if they have not been involved in producing it: so it is particularly important that all those who will be responsible for carrying out the plan should play their part in drawing it up.

Integrating the business and family plans
A recent UK survey showed that only 10 per cent of family company respondents strongly agreed with the statement that their business had a well-developed strategic plan which is completely relevant to and supportive of the family mission. The problem is that in a family business you cannot create a strategic business plan without considering the family's interests. For example, if the family is not committed to the long-term future of the business, or if the management succession issue has not been resolved, the continuity of the business is brought into question – and this obviously has a profound effect on the business plan.

Similarly, human resource issues such as recruitment, remuneration and performance appraisal are particularly problematical in family businesses. From a family perspective, the desire and tendency is to *equalise*: give everyone a job; pay them the same; ignore individual performance. The business need, on the other hand, is to *differentiate*: employ the best talent available and give a job to family members only if they can contribute; establish a management hierarchy; evaluate performance objectively; and reward individuals according to their responsibilities and achievements.

Thus, the family's strategic plan is essential to the development of the business plan. Because of this, and because ensuring the family's commitment is crucial, the family strategic plan should be developed first.

The management plan

To support the implementation and monitoring of the strategic business plan, a separate management plan should be drawn up that sets out operational procedures to translate the business plan into specific goals for the people who are responsible for its implementation. Key elements in the management plan will include:

1. a documented organisational structure and job descriptions;
2. measurable performance goals;
3. an objective performance review and appraisal system;
4. a training and development programme;
5. competency/performance-based remuneration; and
6. monitoring and control methods.

Establishing a crystal-clear organisational structure is vitally important. Changing behaviour patterns in the company, which, as already mentioned, is one of the main objectives of professionalising the business, almost always involves changing its structure. The guiding principle should be that authority and responsibility are to be decentralised to the lowest

Table 4.3 *Organisational structure in strategic management*

- How communication works
- How decisions are made
- How operational rules are established
- How accountability is ensured
- How performance is recognised and rewarded

possible level, and the main structural issues that must be resolved are summarised in Table 4.3.

Like the strategic plan, the structural aspects of the management plan can therefore help companies to focus on some of the more sensitive issues relating to having family in the business. Many MDs of family firms are unwilling or unable to apply the same organisational procedures to family members as they do to employees. As discussed earlier, some owners expect too much from their adult children working in the business, while others do not expect enough; the children themselves may be too dependent or rebellious; or the owner's spouse may assume authority in the business because of their marriage, regardless of ability to contribute. Because issues such as job descriptions, remuneration and performance assessment can be such a rich source of confusion and tension stemming from family involvement in the business, much of the next chapter is devoted to examining the best ways to approach these human resource problems. As far as the present discussion is concerned, they simply emphasise the earlier recommendation that developing a family strategic plan should precede strategic business planning.

Management reporting
Sound controls and timely management reporting make it possible to quantify the results of previous planning and to measure their accuracy, thus providing a foundation for

well-informed decisions concerning any necessary corrective action. So an efficient management reporting system is an essential link in the strategic management chain, and it should possess a number of characteristics:

1. The system must be simple and practical. It should supply information in accordance with management requirements, and in an accessible, easily understood format.
2. The frequency with which information is supplied should be appropriate to the needs of the user. Daily information on debtors may well be necessary for the collections' department but, unless there is a problem, the MD can rely on weekly or monthly reports.
3. Important information should be available quickly. Management's ability to rectify an adverse variance between actual and budgeted expenses, for example, is not helped if details are received two or three months after the event.

Clear and consistent communication

Communication failings can represent a problem in the early product-driven phase of business development. Even when the business is still small enough for the owner to keep all the balls in the air and make all the important decisions – i.e. even when only one person is effectively the source of all knowledge about the business – communication often breaks down because of the pace of entrepreneurial developments and too much secrecy. At this early stage, the problem need not represent a fundamental weakness. But as the business is professionalised and control is decentralised, adequate and precise communication within the organisation becomes central to the management process.

If employees do not receive information that could affect their performance it hinders not only their personal development but also the team-building that is essential to creating a lasting business. Here are some ideas that can help to encourage communication:

1. *Become less secretive.* Objectively examine your fears as well as the information about the business that you regard as highly confidential. Will knowledge about it really be of significant benefit to your competitors, or will your employees really leave if they know there are problems? Similarly, will the work-force all demand shares in the business if they know how fast it is growing, or how big your salary is? The answer to these questions is usually 'no', and the damage caused to the business by excessive secrecy generally far exceeds that caused by a more open policy.

2. *Tell your people about the plan.* Communicate the strategic plan (in full or a summary), and you will probably be astonished at the amount of interest and enthusiasm it generates. Keep employees in touch with developments via regular progress reports (e.g. a newsletter) and organise periodic meetings.

3. *Stimulate communication, and listen.* Think of ways to encourage two-way communication within the organisation – write memos, ask for replies, arrange staff meetings, weekend events, and so on. An atmosphere of trust and candour can only benefit the company. Also, try to cultivate a listening rather than a dominating approach to discussions. Employees asked about the most important quality a good manager can possess will probably say, 'He listens'.

Outside advice and assistance

Outside help can contribute significantly to the strategic management process and to the success potential of the family business. Experienced consultants can act as facilitators in both family and business strategic planning – organising the process, guiding the discussions and providing an objective perspective.

Specialist outsiders can also help in relation to a whole range of other issues, including succession, share ownership, estate planning, acquisitions, family business taxation, training, as well as operational, project and financial management. In addition, many family businesses find it immensely valuable to involve outsiders at board level in their company. Independent, outside directors meeting regularly to advise the company on business policies can often provide an injection of professionalism and objectivity to board discussions, as well as a counterbalance to the introverted stance of many family firms. Professionalising the business means a move into uncharted waters for the management of most family businesses, and this is precisely the sort of area where experienced, outside directors can make a particularly constructive contribution.

Professionalising the business: Key suggestions

> • If a family business is to grow beyond the product- and process-driven development phases, instinctive management must give way to a professionalised approach based on planning and controlling growth using strategic management techniques.
> • The organisation needs to acquire more sophisticated skills that shift management emphasis from control to co-ordination.
> • Successful companies establish clear lines of authority, responsibility and also accountability, and tend to push decision-making responsibilities downwards.
> • The family strategic plan is a core ingredient in the business strategic plan and should be developed first.
> • Communication within the business should be open, timely, and complete enough for employees to be able to do their jobs properly. Many owners need to become less secretive and more willing to share their thinking.

5 Employee Management and Motivation

This chapter examines the effective use of personnel in family businesses. The central problem, once again, concerns the ambiguous position of family firms, forced to inhabit the dangerous no man's land at the border between two different social systems – family and business. The analysis of these systems in Chapter 1 showed how family values and rules of conduct are based on emotional considerations favouring the care and development of the family, while business values and behaviour emphasise performance and results and are based on successfully carrying out tasks.

Conflict between the systems is particularly acute and troublesome in relation to personnel practices: for example, employing family members even though an outsider might be brought in who could do the job better, deciding whether to pay family members a market rate or a family rate for the job, and how to judge their performance. The discussion will therefore centre on the problems family businesses face in the areas of recruitment, remuneration, appraisal and so on, highlighting the difficulties to look out for and suggesting some strategies for coping with them. Next, the sometimes awkward question of non-family employees is examined (especially in relation to managers and middle-managers) – recruitment difficulties, how they fit in, and how to secure the best out of them. Because employee motivation is such an important topic for family members and outsiders alike, the chapter concludes with a

Figure 5.1   *Overlapping systems and human resources*

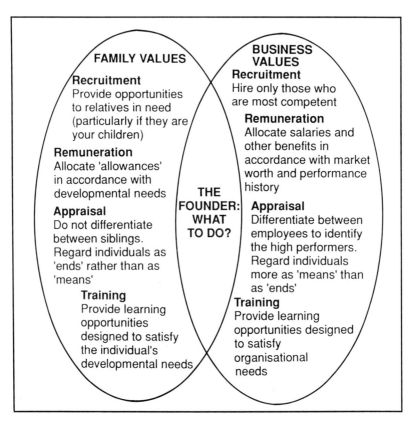

discussion of job satisfaction and incentives, and the ways they can be combined to secure superior performance.

FAMILY BUSINESS PERSONNEL

Figure 5.1, adapted from an illustration used by Ivan Lansberg in an excellent article on human resources in family firms, provides an overview of the clash between family and business values that apply to the main personnel issues in family businesses.[1] These issues and others will be looked at in detail, but the main point to stress here is that the different behavioural standards that apply in the family and business systems are, to a greater or lesser extent, contradictory. The contradictions, and the conflicts they create, are built into the fabric of family businesses and, as with similar problems looked at elsewhere in this book, there are few, if any, easy solutions. Nor does the structural nature of the conflicts reduce the personal impact they can have on the individual who generally suffers their effects most – i.e. the founder. They come with the job, and the psychological stress they engender can severely reduce the founder's ability to manage the family firm effectively.

These conflicts, and what can be done about them, will be examined in relation to the following aspects of personnel management:

1. recruitment;
2. training and development;
3. remuneration;
4. performance appraisal and promotion; and
5. termination and retirement.

Recruitment

Family principles dictate that unconditional help should be provided to family members and other relatives in need. Thus typically, and regardless of ability or expertise, positions of authority within the family business are reserved for family members who, for their part, often feel they have a right to a job

---

[1]Lansberg, I.S. (1983). 'Managing human resources in family firms: The problem of institutional overlap'. *Organizational Dynamics*, Summer, 39–46. Extracts reprinted by permission of the publisher, © 1983, American Management Association, New York. All rights reserved.

in the company. Also, many founders *expect* their adult children to join the family business and commit their working lives to it, notwithstanding the fact that they may lack the aptitude or the talent, or both, to be successful.

"AH DEREK, MY NEPHEW ERNEST...HE'LL BE JOINING THE RESEARCH TEAM ON MONDAY."

This was an issue in one firm visited by our researchers where the youngest son of the present MD had been employed in a number of positions within the company but had not excelled at any of them. The son had been sent to work for other relatives but this was not seen as a permanent solution. The MD was conscious of the issue but could see no clear way to resolve the difficulty. On the one hand he was sensitive to the needs of his son while, on the other, he was aware of the potential harm that could result from the firm carrying a manager not able to make a full contribution.

As far as the standards and values that govern business behaviour are concerned, recruitment policies based on heredity or the provision of a safe haven are, of course, anathema. Business principles demand that only people who are the most competent and suited for the job should be employed. Ignoring these yardsticks and hiring individuals according to their family status represents an obvious threat to the firm's effectiveness and, ultimately, its survival.

It is generally the founder who has to decide whether or not to employ a family member. If his heart is set on establishing a corporate dynasty, the decision will not be difficult. But if he places rather more weight on trying to safeguard the long-term welfare of the enterprise, he may have to face the dilemma of either employing someone not capable of doing the job or facing the wrath of the family if he chooses to employ an outsider.

How to cope, and an approach to a solution

This type of predicament arises in relation to all the personnel management issues discussed in this section. Here is a good place, therefore, to look at coping strategies, together with the basis for a generalised approach to family business personnel problems that can be applied beyond just the recruitment issue. First, however, let's look at how *not* to try and cope.

Figure 5.1 illustrated the founder trapped between the family and business systems, facing powerful but conflicting pressures about the best way to resolve personnel dilemmas. Many owners finding themselves being squeezed in this way opt for one of two strategies. Either they try to find a compromise between the two sets of conflicting forces, or they swing indiscriminately between strict adherence to business principles on some occasions, and family principles on others. But the compromise approach often leads to decisions that are bad for the business, while the second, 'seesaw' strategy produces arbitrary and unpredictable behaviour that is incomprehensible and unsettling as far as both employees and family members are concerned. The two strategies share a common fundamental defect – neither is based on clear and explicit management criteria.

As mentioned at the start of this section, these contradictory pressures are built into the very fabric of family businesses. The most constructive approach for founders, therefore, rather than seeking an essentially unobtainable clear-cut solution, is to settle for trying to develop procedures that recognise and manage the contradictions. An important first step which reduces the stresses produced by the conflicts, and thus increases the founder's ability to manage them, is to understand and accept that they are structural, not personal problems – in short, they 'come with the territory'.

Secondly, as Lansberg suggests,[2] it is helpful to explain and share the problem with both family members and senior management in the business. This shifts the focus of the predicament away from the founder and on to the family business system which, because it is a structural dilemma, is where it belongs. Involving others in this way should stimulate the development of procedures to define and separate family and business issues, encouraging collaborative problem solving among all the parties concerned.

The author goes on to propose that the key to developing effective procedures for managing these contradictions lies in the separation of management and ownership. This involves:

> examining the relatives who work in the firm from two distinct perspectives: an 'ownership' perspective and a 'management' perspective. From an ownership perspective, relatives would be subject to all the norms and principles that regulate family relations; from a management perspective, relatives would be affected by the firm's principles.

In personnel recruitment, the distinction would entail:

> accepting into the firm only those relatives who, on business grounds, were thought to possess the skills needed to

---

[2]Ibid, p.45.

perform effectively on the job. Hence from a management perspective relatives would be treated just as others are treated when they apply for a position. From an ownership point of view, on the other hand, relatives interested in working in the firm would be given the opportunity to acquire the necessary skills required to meet the firm's standards. These opportunities could take many forms, including sponsored apprenticeships in other firms, formal education, training, and so forth. The funds to cover the necessary training expenses would come from the family's assets rather than from the business. In this way relatives could be taken care of in a manner consistent with family principles, without necessarily compromising the firm's sound management standards.[3]

Confusion about who can and who cannot join the company can seriously damage family relationships. As in so many other aspects of family business life, agreeing clear criteria and guidelines that specify when family or business principles are appropriate will go a long way towards reducing the potential for conflict and promoting the effective management of human resources in family firms. The family's agreed position on personnel issues provides an excellent example of the sort of policy statement that should be included in the family strategic plan, discussed in Chapter 3.

In the light of this constructive approach to human resource management issues generally, let's move on to examine how it should apply to the other personnel practices listed at the start of this section.

Training and development
Under family principles, family members should be trained according to what is best for them as individuals. Business norms, on the other hand, are less concerned with the flowering

---

[3]Ibid.

of well-rounded individual personalities – they demand that training and development should be based on learning experiences that improve the individual's ability to contribute to the achievement of organisational objectives. What is best for the individual and what is best for the business do not always coincide.

In addition, the business may well suffer when founders invest the company's resources to provide their offspring with an opportunity for promoting their individual well-being and development. Such laudable family projects can range from paying for a training course through to buying a company for the children to run and, in either case, the exercise may at best be unrelated to promoting business goals, and at worst completely incompatible with them.

Applying the ownership–management distinction, discussed earlier, from a management viewpoint it is important that the training and development of relatives should depend on, and fit in with the firm's needs. If a family member's ambitions are inconsistent with the firm's needs, he or she must choose between employment in the family business or following personal plans using family assets. In other words, from the ownership perspective family members would be entitled to draw on family assets to invest in pursuing their professional objectives outside the family business.

Remuneration

What to pay relatives who work in the family firm also creates difficult problems. In the family system, the guiding norms are that family wealth should either be distributed according to need, or according to principles that are transparently fair. In the case of siblings, for example, fairness is generally taken to mean that resources be allocated equally. But in the business, remuneration should be based on the individual's contribution. It is interesting to note that in a recent UK survey, almost 20 per cent of family firms were willing to admit that family members' salaries were not set at market levels.

The Irish are not comfortable discussing money generally, and personal salary or wage levels in particular. For founders required to talk about remuneration terms with their relatives (especially their children), the word 'discomfort' does not adequately sum up the trauma involved. As a result, what relatives should be paid is generally decided on the basis of an ambiguous combination of principles – some from the family system, some from the business system – and they generate all sorts of tension and inefficiency in the company. Thus we find that some companies pay family members significantly more than the market rate or, more commonly, less than this rate, on the principle that they have an obligation 'to help out'. Other firms pay all family members at the same rate, regardless of their contribution, with the likely result that incompetent relatives stay and competent ones leave the company to earn a fairer salary elsewhere.

In the case of remuneration, the problem-solving approach based on the separation of management and ownership would entail rewarding relatives strictly on the basis of business principles. If desired, the ownership route can be used to boost family members' earnings independent of their role within the company – for example, by way of share dividends rather than a higher salary. Such an arrangement acknowledges the privileges of ownership but preserves a merit-based reward system in the business. Whatever the policy details that are finally chosen, they should be clearly spelled out so that they are understood by all family members inside the business, as well as by those who might be contemplating joining. It is also worth considering the establishment of a salaries' committee of the board. If the committee deals with everyone's salaries, this encourages the feeling that remuneration is being approached in a systematic, even-handed way – a feeling that will be reinforced if the committee includes some non-executive directors among its members.

Performance appraisal and promotion

Most employees want to know what is expected of them and want feedback on how they are doing. If this is carried out constructively, areas that need improvement can be identified and areas of good performance can be reinforced. This, indeed, is the rationale for appraisal in business activity, where individuals are judged on their ability to contribute to the achievement of organisational goals. But, to put it mildly, it is against family principles to apply an objectively derived set of criteria in order to evaluate the worth of family members.

It is hardly surprising, therefore, that founders, facing the unenviable task of having to assess the managerial competence of their offspring or other relatives, suffer serious psychological stress. It is simply not possible for them to do justice to the requirements and norms of both the family and the business. Once again, the effects of this institutional overlap can at least be minimised by clearly distinguishing family (ownership) and business (management) principles. The separation implies that family members working in the business must be subject to evaluation on professional grounds like all other employees. Modern management techniques emphasise the value of self-assessment – individuals evaluating themselves against their own pre-determined performance targets, and discussing the results with employers and colleagues. The process should also include obtaining the views of other employees (peers, superiors and subordinates) in order to reduce the potential for family bias and to promote objectivity. Canvassing opinion in this way is probably best achieved by providing for anonymous responses, perhaps to a regular, standardised questionnaire. Otherwise there is the risk of non-family employees 'covering' for incompetent family members.

A similar type of approach should be considered in relation to establishing a formal policy on job promotion. Decisions on promotion can be entrusted to a special group composed of both family and non-family members where neither side has a majority vote. This group procedure can even be extended to promotion at director level. An objective evaluation and promotion policy brings with it three principal advantages:

1. Appraisals are clearly not based on favouritism.

2. The potential for rivalry and jealousy between both family and non-family employees is reduced.
3. It encourages the development of a much more professionalised managerial climate.

Termination and retirement

Termination is included here for completeness, but really, of course, it is simply the mirror image of the recruitment question considered at the start of this section. From a management perspective it was proposed that relatives should be recruited for a job only if they are competent to do it; thus, they should be dismissed if they do not possess the right skills. So, instead of a predicament over whether or not to employ a family member, owners find themselves having to choose between continuing to employ an incompetent relative, or risking damaging their relationship with the family.

Establishing an objective set of job termination (and retirement) policies is, of course, a major step towards an answer, but this process in itself can involve a battle against family system principles. Defining dismissal and retirement criteria will probably be seen as hostile to the sense of corporate paternalism in most family firms, and this can extend beyond laying down formal guidelines in respect of family members – doing the same for non-family employees is sometimes seen as equally incompatible with the firm's culture. It is nevertheless important that the battle be fought, and won. Failure to address the issue successfully results in all sorts of damaging stresses and inefficiency creeping into the organisation – resentment caused by perceived favouritism, fictional jobs being created for incompetent relatives, and so on.

As regards retirement, even family businesses that do have formal policies often encounter difficulties when family executives simply refuse to adhere to the guidelines. The problem is particularly troublesome in the case of founders who do not easily accept retirement because they believe they are indispensable to the enterprise. Thus they resist pressures to retire that come from potential successors, their wives, or from other family members in the business. The difficulties are highlighted in a great many reported cases in which the sequence of events runs roughly as follows: the MD's retirement date is fixed; succession arrangements are all in place; the company's people, family and non-family, all gather on the appointed Friday evening to mark the event with champagne and speeches; the MD explains all the wonderful things he plans to do to ensure an enjoyable and happy retirement; the following Monday comes and, to everyone's astonishment (although for his successor read 'horror') he is back at his desk as usual, explaining that 'there are one or two things I still need to sort out'.

In Chapter 7 on 'Succession management' this phenomenon is looked at in detail, together with a number of variations on it (for example, the ex-MD, finally installed in his retirement cottage, but using it as a campaign headquarters from which he plots his triumphant return to the office). In the current context, however, the problem serves to emphasise the vital importance of establishing clear-cut, objective criteria for retirement as well as for the other personnel issues examined here. The resulting guidelines may not always be followed, and the system overlap dilemmas may not always be resolved, but thinking about what should happen in these situations, and spelling out the policies so that they are understood by all, will minimise the potential for turmoil. Provided this is achieved, and given the personal atmosphere and sense of belonging and common purpose that predominate in most family businesses, such firms are in a better position to manage human resources and get the most out of them.

NON-FAMILY EMPLOYEES

The sometimes tricky position of non-family employees in family businesses was discussed in broad terms in Chapter 2 – especially their relationship with the family. Here, their role is examined from more of a management perspective.

In the previous section it was proposed that family members

should become managers only if they are sufficiently competent. If it is apparent that no family members could, even after training, meet this requirement, then the firm ought to recruit an outsider. Both the firm and the family will be better off if only the most qualified people get management positions.

But family companies have a problem finding talented outsiders willing to work for them and, once found, they also have a problem in motivating them. For family businesses in which business principles have not been separated from family principles, these problems can be very serious. Qualified outsiders expect to find (and in this case they will probably be right) that nepotism prevails in family companies, and that it will prevent them being given a fair chance. Many have doubts about whether the firm is being run professionally by the family – if it is, why should they be bringing someone in? They will usually be unable to aspire to ownership, or even leadership, their salary will probably lag behind levels obtainable in non-family firms, their decisions may be overruled by family members or, worse, they risk becoming a pawn in some endless family battle.

However, if the company is professionally run and the business–family separation is made, most of these problems disappear, or at least are minimised. The benefits that flow from such a separation were highlighted in the previous section. Managerial positions, for example, cease to be the exclusive preserve of relatives, while remuneration and assessment are more objective. Indeed, the overall result can often make the family business more attractive to capable outsiders than working for a non-family public company. The reasons for this include:

1. New executives can expect quicker exposure to a wide variety of decision-making situations.
2. They often find it much easier to get things done than in a large, dispersed-ownership company.
3. They enjoy the more personal and satisfying working environment to be found in the family firm sector.

4. They value the opportunity to interact with the owner and key decision maker.

The change in the Irish commercial climate in recent years, particularly the increased emphasis on enterprise, has also played its part in making employment in smaller operations more attractive to professional managers.

To sum up, the common denominators of family businesses that enjoy the benefits of dedicated and highly motivated non-family employees are:

- Family and non-family members are recruited and evaluated according to merit – identical, objective standards apply.
- Acceptable career development opportunities are provided for non-family employees, and remuneration is related to economic principles.
- If there are any conflicts between family members, these are not allowed to affect the business.
- A management succession plan has been put in place by the owner, and has been explained to non-family employees.
- The valuable role played by non-family employees in fostering the success of the business is openly acknowledged and rewarded.

Recognition and reward of both family and non-family employees can take many forms, ranging from simple verbal acknowledgement – a pat on the back – through cash bonuses to elaborate performance-linked incentive schemes. They are all aspects of employee motivation that can provide family businesses with superior performance and a competitive edge.

MOTIVATING YOUR EMPLOYEES

There is a common misconception that the best way to motivate employees is with the 'carrot' of financial incentives and the 'stick' of penalising failure. The only advantage to this approach is its simplicity, which is perhaps why it is popular. But if you ask highly motivated employees to explain their motivation they do not usually place pay and benefits at the top of the list: more likely they will respond, 'Because I love my job.'

Pay and benefits are often even less likely to represent key motivating factors for family managers, who sometimes tend to describe their motivation in terms of duty, either to their parents or to other family members. They see their role as a custodial one of preserving the firm for the next generation and, as a result, are unlikely to make good managers.

Getting the best performance

The value of a highly motivated work-force (at all levels) is impossible to underestimate, and the carrot and stick method will never achieve the desired result because it is based on a misunderstanding of what it is that stimulates employees to superior performance. Enjoying the carrot and fearing the stick may well ensure that people work hard enough to keep their salary cheques coming, but someone who is afraid is unable to perform at the limits of their capabilities.

The approach relies exclusively on external influences and ignores the crucial fact that motivation must come from within – in other words, there must be self-motivation. The important areas of concern therefore revolve around personal factors like achievement, recognition, how satisfying is the job itself, the need for responsibility and personal development. These are true motivating forces, whereas external matters such as company policy, organisational structure, salary levels and incentive schemes do not in themselves motivate, although they are important in helping to kindle self-motivation and to encourage it.

The objective, therefore, is to develop ways to help release the natural desire of employees to do their best work. What we are seeking is not employees working hard enough to get by, but employees working to their limits and putting in that extra effort that comes from really caring about what they do. It is this little bit extra that is the hallmark of a highly motivated work-force, and of imaginative, innovative and outward-looking companies. Here are some practical steps you can take to foster motivation:

- Encourage employees to use their own judgement and to improvise. For example, establish work groups in which employees decide on the details of how a job should be done.
- As well as authority, give employees responsibility for results. For example, structure tasks so that employees can follow them through in a logical sequence from beginning to end, and so that they assume complete responsibility.
- Communicate goals clearly and make it understood that the employee is accountable. Keeping people informed helps them to feel respected and also helps them to solve problems.
- Make work rules flexible so that individuals fit them to their own needs. This reduces the emphasis on less important factors, like, for example, when a particular job is done, and helps to focus on the central issue of results.

INCENTIVE SCHEMES

There is a huge variety of strategies and schemes that can help create and support the vital ingredient of self-motivation. It would be out of place in this book to describe and analyse them all in detail. What follows, however, is a summary of the pros and cons of the most important types of scheme, and an outline of how each works. Readers who then wish to obtain more information about particular schemes, especially their tax treatment, should refer to more specialist texts. First, however, let's look at some general considerations underlying the introduction of a scheme. The section is particularly applicable to cash incentives.

Designing an incentive scheme

Before examining the details of particular incentive schemes, it is imperative to have a clear understanding of what will and will not work within your own organisation. Designing a scheme can be split into seven constituent stages (see Table 5.1) which should each be considered in turn.

1. Why introduce a scheme?

Performance is not simply a matter of motivation. It will also depend on the ability of the employees and their understanding of the tasks. All three factors – motivation, ability and clarity of task – must be present, and must be kept in balance if performance is to be maximised. There is little point in providing incentives if employees do not have the necessary ability or do not understand what they are required to do.

The next point is to consider the likely effect any scheme may have on performance. This will depend on both the scope within the business for performance improvement (*headroom*), and the

Table 5.1 *Scheme design stages*

Stage	Comment
1. Why introduce a scheme?	There may be no need
2. Identify your objectives	What are you hoping to achieve?
3. Select the participants	Who do you need to provide with incentives?
4. Choose the performance measure	Pick a measure that matches the scheme objectives
5. Scheme design	Consider the practical implications
6. Launch	Communicate
7. Post-launch	Monitor

scope within the organisation for the employees to influence that performance (*leverage*). Obviously, incentive schemes will achieve the greatest results in high headroom (e.g. a rapidly growing business), high leverage (e.g. top management) situations. Conversely, there may be little or no point in introducing a scheme into a low headroom, low leverage situation.

2. Identifying your objectives

Incentive schemes must be tailored to meet the corporate objectives and ethos of the company to which they relate. It is, however, highly unlikely that one can ever find a scheme that does not have unfortunate side-effects. This is because most companies will have a series of goals, many of which may prove incompatible. For example, increasing profits and raising the level of capital investment are two corporate goals likely to feature on most firms' priority lists. But if employees or management are paid performance-related bonuses there may be a disincentive to invest in capital projects for fear that it would depress current profits.

In practice, the best solution is for the directors or senior management to refine their list of goals down to, say, five core objectives. It is then up to the scheme designer to devise a scheme that will motivate employees to meet as many of these core objectives as possible.

3. Selecting the participants

There is generally no point in including in a scheme those employees whose contribution to achieving corporate objectives is likely to be minimal or non-existent. There may, however, be a place for a company-wide scheme where, for example, there is a lack of overall cohesion that senior management wishes to eliminate. Otherwise, a set of different schemes should be set up, each directly targeted at a defined group of employees.

It is also important to evaluate how a scheme will affect and interact with existing pay structures, as well as future pay increases and pension arrangements.

4. Choosing the performance measure

The performance measure selected should normally be one that the employee can influence directly. Put at its simplest, the target for a salesman would therefore relate to sales, whereas the target for a manager would relate to some measure of profits. Thus, there should be a direct linkage between the efforts employees put in and the rewards they get out.

Some of the most common measures are sales, profits, length of service, return on capital employed, share price, earnings per share and net asset value. The choice among these, or any other measures, depends on analysis of which ones most closely relate to your company's core objectives.

It is important for employees to be involved in the choice of performance measure so that they understand how it is to be defined. Also, if incentive payments are to be calculated by reference to performance against target, the target should be realistic and achievable. Targets which are either too high or too low will not help motivate employees to perform.

5. Scheme design

Once the broad outline and parameters of the scheme have been determined, the next stage is to ensure that the documentation setting out the scheme rules is as comprehensive as possible. It should make provision for most conceivable eventualities, including:

- definition of terms;
- duration of the scheme;
- calculation of incentive payments;
- floors and ceilings (i.e. minimum and maximum payments);
- distribution of payments;
- payment timing;
- cessation of employment;
- what will happen if there is a change of company control; and
- amendment.

6. Launch

Any incentive scheme is only as good as it is *perceived to be* by the employees, and the keynote is communication. The introduction of the scheme must be supported by all interested parties, the rules must be explained clearly and the benefits understood.

7. Post-launch

The final stage of designing an incentive scheme is the monitoring of the scheme post-launch in order to ensure that it is used to its greatest potential. Targets should be prominently displayed so that all employees are aware of their position and its implications, and the importance of the scheme should be emphasised at regular appraisal meetings.

Non-cash schemes

Non-cash incentives can be more powerful than cash payments in helping to motivate employees. Cash is largely invisible and soon forgotten, whereas non-cash incentives such as a paid holiday or a company car tend to live on in the employee's memory.

It is important to get the balance right, however: few employees will appreciate being rewarded entirely in non-cash ways, and any non-cash element within an incentive package should be carefully monitored to ensure that it does not have a negative effect.

Notwithstanding the substantial increase in the taxation of company cars in recent years, they remain one of the most widespread and the most visible of all fringe benefits. (As with most of the incentives mentioned in this chapter, the taxation of company cars is extremely complex and readers should take professional advice concerning the detailed tax treatment of any incentive scheme.)

Other non-cash incentives include voucher schemes (for example, retail store or holiday vouchers), staff conferences held overseas, medical insurance, cheap loans, luncheon facilities and accommodation.

Pensions in incentive planning

Pensions are by far the most widely used form of fringe benefit, and many directors and employees in Ireland belong to a company pension scheme. Despite this, historically company pensions have not enjoyed a very high profile, although fundamental changes to the pension regime in recent years (especially in the area of job mobility and 'portable' pensions) have resulted in employees becoming increasingly pension-aware.

The two main types of pension scheme are final salary and money purchase schemes. Final salary schemes provide a specific level of benefits at retirement, based on a percentage of earnings for each year of service. Because they are designed to provide specific benefits for a large and ever-changing number of people at retirement, the costing of final salary schemes is complex and requires the services of an actuary. Under money purchase schemes, on the other hand, the employer can elect to pay a specified monetary contribution for the employee (expressed as a percentage of salary or, indeed, a particular amount). In this way, the employer remains in control of the cost of the scheme.

In examining pensions as part of an incentive package, companies should consider carefully all the relative attractions and disadvantages of the two main types of scheme, as well as the increasing variety of other options and 'add-ons' that are becoming available in this fast moving field.

Share incentives

The increasing use of shares and share options to attract, retain and motivate employees was, without doubt, one of the most important developments in incentive planning in the 1980s. However, many family businesses limit share ownership to family members.

Let's therefore look at two possibilities that may provide some room for manoeuvre in situations where the family is keen to avoid diluting its stake in the business, but where key employees may be pressing to receive a 'piece of the action'.

Phantom share options

In reality, a phantom share option scheme is little more than a bonus plan dressed up to look like a share scheme. The employee is granted a phantom option to buy shares at the current value, and can exercise the option during a set period of time specified in the scheme rules. He or she is treated as having sold the shares at the valuation ruling at the date of exercise. The company pays the employee a cash bonus equal to the gain made on the phantom option.

Thus, a phantom scheme is a straightforward concept and is simple to administer. Shareholder approval is not required and the company should normally obtain a tax deduction in respect of the bonus paid on the exercise of the option. It is, however, a cash scheme and will therefore have a negative impact on both cash flow and profits. The bonus is treated as income in the hands of the recipient, and income tax and PRSI contributions are due in the normal way.

Restricted shares

The second possibility is to issue employees with real shares, but ones that carry special voting or transfer restrictions.

If, for example, the family is not particularly concerned about the effect of issuing shares from the point of view of diluting the value of its holding, but is worried about loss of control, it can offer employees non-voting, or limited voting shares. These are identical to all other shares except they carry no rights (or restricted rights) to vote at general meetings. In most cases, the company may feel it appropriate to enfranchise the employee shares in the event of a public flotation, although professional advice should always be taken on the taxation implications of varying the rights of employee-held shares.

A variation on this is to issue shares which, once again, are identical to all the others except, in this case, they are required to be offered back to the company when the employee leaves, or before they can be sold. This does, however, give the employee all the rights of a minority shareholder, and sometimes families are reluctant to subject the business to this exposure.

Many family companies arrive at the conclusion that if they are going to reach a situation from which they will be able to attract and motivate professional managers then they must be prepared to release, in an unrestricted form, at least a small proportion of the equity in their company.

CONCLUSIONS

An unstructured approach to managing employee resources can work in companies that are still small enough for the owner to be involved personally in all aspects of the business. But if you have employees who must operate independently, then more organised methods, along the lines discussed in this chapter, will almost certainly be needed.

Inventiveness and flexibility – hallmarks of the best family businesses – need not be sacrificed by the introduction of a more structured approach. Indeed, implemented carefully, an employee management and motivation programme ought to help you make the most of these strengths.

Employee management and motivation: Key suggestions

- Clear and explicit management criteria must be drawn up relating to personnel issues and family members.
- The contradictory forces are best managed by maintaining a firm distinction between ownership considerations (under which family employees are subject to family norms) and management considerations (under which they are required to submit to the company's principles).
- Family employees should thus be rewarded and promoted in line with their contribution to the business, and their performance should be evaluated regularly and objectively within a system that applies to all staff.
- Work in order to attract and motivate high quality non-family employees, and openly recognise and reward their contribution.

Key suggestions (contd.)

> • Motivation comes from within. Encourage employees to use their own judgement and give them responsibility for results. Communicate your goals clearly and make it understood that the employee is accountable.
>
> • Before adopting a particular type of incentive scheme, define carefully what you wish to achieve, and make sure the scheme will operate effectively in your organisation.

6 Boardroom Resources

Perhaps one of the most striking characteristics that distinguishes the best family businesses is that they generally operate with a strong, independent board of directors. This is not intended to mean that they have a separate or supervisory board on the European model, but that the single board of directors, charged with overseeing the company's operations, includes independent, non-family outsiders.

The fact implies acceptance of the proposition that outside assistance can contribute enormously to the success potential of the family business – a conclusion that does not always come easily to family business founders. The founder's character is often incompatible with bringing in outsiders – many, indeed, actually attribute their success to pursuing their own objectives, in their own way, and paying scant attention to what others have to say. It should come as no surprise, therefore, that introducing outside directors and thus moving towards a more accountable system of corporate governance is seen as an unpalatable option by a great many founders.

THE FICTIONAL BOARD

As a result, the boards of private, family-owned companies normally consist of family members and they usually confine their activities to the minimum necessary to fulfil statutory obligations. In effect, they operate as a rubber stamp and exercise few, if any, of the serious management functions or the authority that can be vested in a board.

The typical family firm MD's view of independent directors is, 'I created and built the company on my own, I'm the controlling shareholder, and I make all the decisions: why would outsiders want to be involved with my company, and why would I want them?' The last point is usually the crux of the matter, with the founder taking a suitably jaundiced view about establishing an independent board of directors to which he would be accountable and which would be 'looking over his shoulder' and questioning his operation of the business.

This is consistent with the common misconception that only big, public companies should have broadly based, independent boards. Many owners of family businesses, who tend to operate in an atmosphere of informality and secrecy, are less than comfortable with the thought of sharing confidential business

"YOU HAVE, OF COURSE, GOT COMPLETE AUTHORITY TO HAVE EVERYTHING APPROVED BY ME."

information and airing difficult family issues. But this is part of the price that must be paid if the benefits of an independent board are to be obtained. Generally, the problem for founders is not that this price is too high, but that they do not fully understand how valuable an independent board of directors can be.

Making the transition

Establishing an independent board of directors is probably crucial for the vast majority of family businesses, if they are to secure long-term success. This does not mean, however, that every family business is ready to introduce an independent board. Not all firms would obtain enough benefits from such a move to justify the effort and cost involved. In deciding if such justification exists, consider the following questions:

1. Is the MD committed to making the idea work?
2. Is it a growing, maturing company rather than a one-man business?
3. Is the business substantial enough so that shareholder and operational issues can be easily distinguished from one another?
4. Will the long-term guidance and input from an independent board complement and add to the contribution available from existing professional advisers?
5. Does the business have sufficient resources to implement and take advantage of an independent board's recommendations?

Of all these questions, the first is the most important. Independent boards can only be effective when the MD has the confidence to accept a small reduction in his power and control over the business, and is willing to subject his stewardship to examination by outsiders. There will be little room for the aura of operational secrecy beloved by many family businesses. The MD need not bare his soul and tell the board absolutely everything, but he must keep it sufficiently well informed to do its job. The delicate relationship between the MD and an independent board has been summed up well in an American report on the subject:[1]

> Unless he believes in this concept and is willing to submit to board recommendations, the independent board cannot succeed in helping to develop the business. This does not mean the [MD] must relinquish all control. There may be times when he may find it necessary to exercise the prerogative of a major shareholder and make decisions contrary to the board. Board members will generally accept this, but they must believe that their opinions are valued and that their viewpoints have an impact on the business. An effective board should probe, challenge and offer recommendations in an atmosphere of mutual respect that is supportive rather than adversarial. This balancing act can only exist among mature people who are willing to subordinate their sensitivities to the good of the company.... The board members have a final weapon if they believe that the [MD] is not willing to accept direction. They can resign. They never asked for the job in the first place.

So acquiring the benefits of experienced advisers in the form of an independent board does not limit the MD's flexibility or ultimate authority as owner. Also, while an effective board may require more formal management procedures, these often represent needed disciplines rather than bureaucracy. Family members, active in the day-to-day running of the business, are unlikely to spend precious time preparing detailed reports and analyses when they themselves will be the only readers.

---

[1]'Creating a board of directors: When success demands too much'. *L&H Perspective*, Volume 12 (1986), No.1, 1–5.

EFFECTIVE, WORKING BOARDS

The principal responsibilities of an independent, working board of directors are to establish corporate policy and oversee management performance. The MD is responsible for routine operations, but should submit policy issues and important decisions for board consideration and determination. These include, for example:

- changes to the scope or nature of the company's operations;
- overall strategic planning;
- approving individual strategies in areas such as marketing, production, investment and financial management;
- changes to the company's organisational structure; and
- major corporate decisions, such as selling the business or a significant portion of its assets, mergers, acquisitions and large investments.

Overseeing management performance is the second important board responsibility. Duties in this area include:

- monitoring the effectiveness of management in carrying out corporate objectives;
- planning for management succession; and
- setting management remuneration levels.

Clearly, a number of these corporate policy and management responsibilities can involve some sensitive family questions that many founders are reluctant to face up to – in particular, succession, organisational structure, job definitions and remuneration of family members. But these are, of course, all issues on which the unemotional and objective viewpoint of an independent board can be especially helpful.

Because the board will be involved in helping the family to

resolve its problems, it is important that board members establish a relationship with the family. Its role should not be seen as institutionalised arbitration in family squabbles, but if the board has the family's confidence and respect it can be very valuable in helping to defuse potentially dangerous situations. A vivid illustration of this is provided in cases where the MD has suddenly died or become disabled. Rather than the unprepared family being saddled with responsibility for the business, there are many examples of the board taking over, if necessary hiring a professional manager, and the business continuing in an orderly way with the support of the family until one of the owner's children is ready to assume leadership.

NON-EXECUTIVE DIRECTORS

It is possible for non-executive directors to bring a new dimension of experience and forthright objectivity that is usually not found among family members or employees. How to go about selecting non-executive directors is discussed later in this section but, typically, they tend to be people who have made their career with a large public company – often a multinational – reaching perhaps the divisional director level and opting for early retirement at 55. They will not want to take on huge commitments but, rather than sitting at home, the idea of attending board meetings six or twelve times a year and using their huge store of knowledge and experience to help a smaller company is often very appealing. Such outside directors can make an enormous contribution (at minimal cost). Particular benefits include:

1. objective and seasoned guidance from successful business people;
2. an unbiased sounding-board for family-owned business problems, such as succession;
3. mediation (*not* decision making), helping the family to resolve any disagreements and reduce emotional stresses;

4. specialised expertise that may not be available internally; and
5. a network of contacts that can be mobilised on behalf of the firm. This often covers areas such as potential sources of new business, capital, connections in industry and government, as well as international contacts.

Less tangibly, a good non-executive director can also act as a catalyst, pushing for significant shifts in corporate conduct or objectives that may be beyond the scope and imagination of the inside directors (e.g. acquisitions, revamping the senior personnel, going public, and so on). Overall, he or she should be the informed critic of management, making sure that it thinks and plans.

Selecting the right directors
It is vital to form a clear idea of the sort of blend of personality, talent and experience that will be of most benefit to your company. In general terms, you will want directors who are bright, logical, analytical, honest and well respected. They should be prepared to stand up for their opinions and be a ready source of constructive advice. Personal chemistry is very important – there must be mutual respect and rapport. It is no use if either the MD or the director is liable to take umbrage in the face of criticism from the other. Give and take is essential on both sides if the board is to perform effectively.

Another key consideration is that the skills, experience and temperament of a non-executive director must complement those already in the company. Generally, it is not a good idea to take on someone whose main experience is in the same business as your own, because you will not get the best out of them. But if you are looking to strengthen the firm's financial expertise, consider candidates with a banking or venture capital background. If marketing has proved a persistent weakness it may be that you will benefit most from taking on someone from a reputable advertising or public relations agency. Seek a balance that will introduce some new and valuable skills to your business.

Some MDs shy away from recruiting retired people as non-executive directors. Although they may have the time and experience to make a valuable contribution, if they have been away from business life for a while it can be very easy to lose touch. Also, a candidate whose principal concern is to top up their pension with directors' fees may not display the sort of detached, objective perspective you are seeking. Similarly, employing professional advisers like your accountant or solicitor may be questionable on the grounds of objectivity.

Once you have drawn up a profile of the type of director you need, the next step is to find him, or her, and this is not always easy. The legal responsibilities (and potential liabilities) of directors are becoming more onerous all the time, and the ideal candidates are often busy, successful people who are unlikely to be bowled over by the relatively nominal fees that you can offer. On the other hand, many highly qualified people accept directorships and find they provide a rewarding experience. Becoming an important influence in shaping the destiny of a growing, successful firm can be a very stimulating experience.

A number of organisations keep registers of people who are willing to take on non-executive directorships. The IMI Boardroom and the Institute of Directors (Ireland) offer a fully fledged appointments service, while the major banks, venture capital groups, accountants and recruitment consultants also generally keep lists. Personal contacts are another possibility, but be careful about choosing close friends or people who do business with your company – they may not have the objectivity and independence you need.

Finally, remember that the first selection may be particularly important because their calibre and experience will tend to set the standard as far as later candidates are concerned.

Board practices
Establishing written guidelines setting out how the board should function is often a good idea. These will obviously be

subject to change once the board is formed, but they serve to help you clarify your expectations as well as evidencing your seriousness of purpose, thus helping in the recruitment of board candidates. The role and operational rules of the board should be defined in the guidelines, and information about directors' terms of office and fees should also be included.

It is consistent with the psychology of why outside directors agree to serve at all that their fees should represent a serious gesture of appreciation rather than performance-based remuneration. Fees payable will depend on factors such as the size of the company, the nature of its operations and the frequency of board meetings.

PROFESSIONAL ADVISERS

Outside professional advisers (lawyers, accountants, bankers, grant advisers, and so forth) can contribute significantly to the professionalisation and the success potential of the family business. Chosen wisely, and used properly, they can bring an extra dimension of competence, experience and objectivity to issues that concern both the business and the family.

The trouble is that most family businesses start off with local advisers – often small firms, chosen with cost as a primary consideration – who become involved in setting up the business. A local branch bank manager may have lent the founder some money, a solicitor filed the appropriate forms with Companies Office, and an accountant prepared the first statutory accounts and perhaps helped to set up the bookkeeping system and dealt with the founder's personal tax. This team usually works well until the business begins to grow and requires some specialist services as well as a more sophisticated general service. For example, taxation advice may be needed in relation to a complex transaction, the company may want to establish foreign bank accounts or obtain legal advice on the terms of an international contract. The time arrives when the original advisers can no longer cope – the business they are advising has outgrown them. But because families tend to be loyal and want to support people who have supported them in the early years, there is often a huge reluctance to contemplate a change.

Some family businesses with advisers who are out of their depth take a 'middle course' of introducing a larger firm to see them through a particular, one-off transaction, and then they revert to the original firm. But this generally indicates misplaced loyalty. The company gets the benefit of a capable contribution in relation to the transaction, but the contribution is in a vacuum. The business returns to what is probably an inadequate general service relative to its size and aspirations, and forgoes the benefits of establishing a continuing relationship with a larger firm that is now much more appropriate to the increasing scope of its operations and prospects.

It is important, therefore, to evaluate periodically your relationships with outside professional advisers. Visiting them regularly is a good idea, even if there are no immediate problems. Keep them in touch with what is going on and with your plans. Challenge them to come up with new and creative ideas – if your advisers can only help you on the routine aspects of their field and never make imaginative, thought-provoking suggestions about your business, this is a clear sign that it is time for a change.

Consultants

Consultants do not enjoy a glowing reputation among small to medium-sized businesses generally and, because of their special problems only now beginning to be properly understood, among family businesses in particular. There is a common belief that consultants are excellent at 'examining your watch and telling you the time' – in other words, in providing you with an erudite compilation of your problems but little if anything in the way of constructive advice about how you should go about solving them.

Yet, when you do not have the expertise within the company for a specific task, it often makes sense to engage a good consultant to help. You do not add them to your payroll and, once their job is completed and they leave, if they have been effective you enjoy a long-term benefit that would not otherwise have been possible. Before you engage consultants, check their professional credentials, and talk to others who have used their services. Insist that the scope of the engagement and the fee arrangement be spelled out clearly in writing in advance. As with most things, but particularly with consultants, you get what you pay for. The general rule is to seek the very best your company can afford. There is a range of government grants available that can help to defray the costs of consultants for smaller companies, and it is important that companies take advantage of the various government initiatives in this field.

Good professional consultants are to be found specialising in virtually every facet of commercial activity. There are industry specialists covering, for example, the agribusiness or printing industries, consultants who aim to analyse and solve particular operational problems (e.g. production control), as well as management specialists, expert in areas like strategic business planning or the introduction of computerised systems. It is in this management category that skills particularly valuable to family businesses are to be found.

Family business needs

Specialists can help resolve intra-family rivalries, for example, by assisting in the establishment of objective family member evaluation procedures, family wealth allocation and fair remuneration principles. A family business consultant can also help to develop and implement your family strategic plan. Similarly, the questions of share ownership and estate planning are complex and often fraught with emotion, and specialist advice can minimise both tax liabilities and the potential for family disagreements.

In addition, the family can call in an expert to help with succession or changes to the management structure to ensure continuity in the future. Succession represents a major, sometimes fatal hurdle for family businesses, and one should not assume that the problems that surround it will resolve themselves, or that they will be easy to handle.

CONCLUSIONS

To grow beyond the one-man business stage, a firm must make use of outside expertise. The transition is not an easy one. As the company becomes larger and more complex, the foundations have to be laid for a more structured, less centralised organisation. The task is significantly more difficult for family than for non-family businesses. Without some outside input into the firm, they are all too easily prone to become introverted, inflexible, and uncompetitive.

Boardroom resources: Key suggestions

- Establishing an independent board of directors is probably crucial for the vast majority of family businesses if they are to achieve long-term success.
- Such a board brings objectivity and experience to operational and policy deliberations, and imposes important disciplines by requiring MDs to articulate and justify their plans.
- The board should establish a close relationship with the family. It can play an important, impartial role supporting the family and helping it to resolve problems and difficulties.
- Non-executive directors can be especially valuable to family-owned companies, providing seasoned guidance, specialised expertise, and networking connections.
- Outside advisers can contribute significantly to professionalising the business. Their selection should be based on competence and their performance periodically reviewed.

Chapters 1 to 6: Work to be done

- Maintain a positive, proactive problem-solving outlook on family relationships.
- Avoid procrastination.
- Generate the right kind of leadership.
- Manage risk.
- Give time to family relationships.
- Put the needs of the family first when necessary.
- Trust the family.
- Build inter-generational teamwork.
- Innovate and change.
- Attract and keep a high-quality management team.
- Plan long term, maintaining energy, commitment and vision.

Case Histories

PROFESSIONALISING THE BUSINESS

At a company where the founder died suddenly, his daughter who had been acting as his secretary found herself in charge. She had to decide whether to sell the firm, bring in an outside manager, or manage it herself. She had strong views about the firm's role in the community and of its duty to employees, and felt that no one outside the family could have the same sense of this. Wanting the family name to remain with the firm, she managed it herself.

Her convictions resulted in a management style of benevolent paternalism similar to that of her father. In consequence, no major changes to the way the business was run were made during her period of control, her concerns being more directed towards maintaining the firm's standing in the community.

On her retirement, she appointed her nephew (who was the founder's grandson) as her successor. Initially, the nephew felt bound to continue the style of his predecessors. However, following a major flood at the company's premises, he began to feel a greater sense of his own ownership and a desire to take the business in his own direction.

His aim has been to transform the firm's culture to one of active participation for employees and respect for individuals. To this end, in the 1980s he introduced flexible working hours which resulted in a need for employees to clock in and out.

Flexitime was extended to all employees and now everyone, including shop floor staff, office workers and the MD clock in at the same clock. In addition, to emphasise the importance of the factory floor to all employees, he placed a new car park in a position which results in all employees crossing the factory floor to reach their offices. He also introduced profit-sharing and share option schemes for employees, with a view to releasing to them up to 20 per cent of the family's equity. The company continues to grow and is an extremely successful business with highly motivated employees.

The case illustrates the need for management to ensure they are not stifled by their predecessor's style. It also highlights the benefits of professionalising the business by not allowing family issues to dominate management policy.

BUILDING CONSENSUS

This case concerns a family business established by a husband and wife team. The couple each owned 50 per cent of the company which, after an initial period of profitable trading, began to decline as a result of marital difficulties.

It was suggested that the management be strengthened by the appointment of a non-executive chairman, and a suitable candidate was found whose personality enabled him to cope with the couple. He was able to guide the husband and wife into a separation of roles within the company, with each performing functions for which they were particularly suited. As a result of this, the business began to thrive once again, and the clearly defined management structure helped in the recruitment of extra management talent.

The couple's relationship is now probably better than it has ever been, and this improvement has been reflected in the company's results.

PART III

THE NEXT GENERATION

7 Succession Management

Only 24 per cent of family businesses survive as such through to the second generation, and only 14 per cent make it beyond the third. Sometimes the firm will have been sold or wound up as part of the family's planned and commercially sensible exit from the business. More often it will have collapsed or declined because of a failure to manage the complex and emotion-laden issue of succession from one generation to the next.

This chapter examines the numerous difficulties caused by such transitions and the powerful forces arrayed against successful succession planning. The aim is to help family business people understand the problems and to cope with succession by analysing all the options, explaining the importance of preparation and planning, and by providing practical guidelines on ensuring that the change is accomplished as smoothly and as advantageously as possible.

Transitions from the second generation onwards will not be overlooked but, as the family firm mortality statistics indicate, the discussion must focus on the succession dilemma facing business founders. In any case, much of what will be said is equally applicable to succession between later generations, although they usually face fewer problems since, by definition, the family has already successfully negotiated at least one transition.

Figure 7.1 *The founder's options*

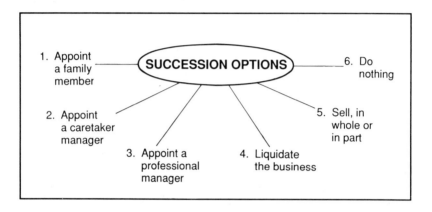

THE NATURE OF THE PROBLEM

Succession confronts the founder of a family business with a complex set of options. For present purposes, these are illustrated in broad terms in Figure 7.1. They will, however, be examined in detail both later in this chapter and, as regards the various alternatives covered by the business sale option, in Chapter 9.

Each option carries its own distinctive set of advantages, disadvantages, opportunities and threats. Also, the scope and impact of these will vary from one family business to another depending on, for example:

- The availability of potential family and non-family successors who are willing and able to carry on the business.
- The needs of the family (for example, whether cash needs to be extracted from the business to provide for the founder's retirement).
- The personal and corporate taxation consequences of the different options.

- The health and size of the business.
- The general commercial and business environment at the time of succession.

The first option of appointing a family member to succeed is particularly attractive as far as most founders are concerned, although options two and three also involve retaining direct control over the business. Option four entails selling off all the company's assets, paying its outstanding debts, and dismissing the work-force. It also involves substantial expenses and is unlikely to result in the best price being obtained.

If possible, some form of sale as a going concern (option five) is likely to recover more value from the business. Alternatives within this option include a trade sale (i.e. an outright sale of the whole business for cash), which may be particularly appealing where no suitable successors can be found, or a flotation can be the best answer if external capital to finance growth is a priority. Similarly, a management buy-out (a sale by the founder to the existing management team, which may include family members) can offer a compromise between transferring the shares to the family and an outright trade sale.

Finally, the founder may simply avoid planning for succession by adopting the 'Do nothing' option, and it is here that we encounter the central paradox. It is the most costly and destructive of all the options, yet it is by far the most popular.

THE CHALLENGE OF SUCCESSION

We are all mortal and it follows that, in order to safeguard the continuity and vitality of the business, owners should regard planning for succession and making sure that it takes place as smoothly and efficiently as possible, as one of their key responsibilities. It is particularly strange, therefore, that despite the logic of this apparently natural transition, as well as the compelling business and family reasons for planning succession, the 'Do nothing' option is the one founders most frequently adopt.

In the case of one family business talked to in research for this book, the founder had a flair for practical innovation and a real love of the business which he ran for 30 years almost as an extension of himself; to customers and the work-force he was the company. He could not conceive of anyone else being able to run it in his place. Wanting something to pass on to his children, he looked into selling the company but could not find a good enough offer. Then in his 60s, and still very much in control of the company, he fell ill unexpectedly and died soon after. There was no natural successor. His two daughters had little involvement in the business, and his two sons (the youngest just out of university) felt totally unprepared to take over. They had no experience of managing the company at that level, nor did they have a clear picture of how the company worked.

In general terms, therefore, the alternatives are quite stark. Succession may be an organised and gradual process, in which case a trained successor grows into the role under the owner's supervision and guidance; or, instead, it takes place abruptly and unexpectedly when the owner becomes ill or dies, in which case an unprepared family member suddenly finds the job forced upon them. Some of the main reasons why the second scenario unfortunately tends to predominate are examined in the next section. At this preliminary stage, however, a helpful context for the discussion that follows is provided by some interesting US research by Jeffrey Sonnenfeld of Harvard on the ways in which different types of founder leave their business. He discovered that the style of their exit is critical in determining how effectively the next generation is able to manage the family business.[1]

Sonnenfeld concluded that departure styles can be grouped into four categories, which he called monarchs, generals, ambassadors, and governors. The main characteristics of each

---

[1]Sonnenfeld, J. (1988). *The hero's farewell: What happens when CEOs retire*. New York: Oxford University Press (and published in the UK in 1989).

Table 7.1 *Four exit styles*

1. Monarchs	Do not leave office until they are decisively forced out through death or an internal palace revolt.
2. Generals	Are forced out of office, but plot their return, and quickly come back out of retirement to 'save' the business.
3. Ambassadors	Leave office gracefully and frequently serve as post-retirement mentors.
4. Governors	Rule for a limited term of office, retire, and switch to other vocational outlets.

group are summarised in Table 7.1. Monarchs aim to 'die in the saddle' and, until they do, will only be forced out by a revolutionary uprising within the company. This revolt can take the form of ultimatums, the resignations of senior managers, or action by the board of directors. Generals also leave as a result of force, but they immediately begin plotting their return, swiftly coming back from retirement to rescue the company from the real or imagined inadequacy of their successor.

The last two categories, ambassadors and governors, have some rather more positive departure characteristics. When the time is right, ambassadors do not face huge difficulties in managing their personal withdrawal from the business. Also, rather than isolating themselves from the company they tend to become its mentor, often remaining on the board in an advisory capacity, and scrupulously avoiding any interference with the autonomy of their successor. Tom Watson of IBM, for example, after a heart attack at 57, instituted a retirement age of 60 throughout the company, and served as a mentor to the board until his death. Governors, on the other hand, after making a quite graceful and decisive exit from the business, entirely shift their attention to other vocational outlets. After retirement, they maintain little, if any contact with the firm. This style is becoming more common because people are tending to live longer and many are recognising the opportunities for second careers, particularly in entrepreneurial roles. The trend is important because it offers the succeeding generation in governor-controlled companies much more room for manoeuvre than would otherwise be the case.

Describing these four types of exit style is rather like holding up a mirror in which founders might recognise some of their own qualities. They may not always like what they see, but the process is a good first step in beginning to understand the psychological factors that make the succession issue such a difficult one to confront.

Failure to address succession used to be put down to a combination of the entrepreneur's instinctive desire to keep control of his creation, as well as a natural aversion to planning. To an extent this is true, but we are now beginning to appreciate that the reasons are much more subtle and complex. A variety of compelling forces are operating within the founder, the firm and the family, all directed against succession planning.

RESISTANCE TO SUCCESSION PLANNING

In any discussion of the factors that conspire to reduce the likelihood of planning for succession, it is necessary to refer to the pioneering research in this area by Professor Ivan Lansberg at Yale. He identified a whole range of obstacles to succession planning, categorising them into those connected with the founder, the family, the employees, and the general environment in which the firm operates.[2]

---

[2]See, in particular, Lansberg, I.S. (1988). *The succession conspiracy: Mapping resistance to succession planning in first generation family firms.* Yale School of Organization and Management, Working Paper A70.

The founder

The founder is, in most cases, the individual who created the business from nothing and, more than anyone else connected with the firm, faces powerful psychological deterrents to planning his retirement.

Fear of death. Few people find it easy to come to terms with their own mortality, and this is particularly so in the case of entrepreneurs. Their success is usually driven by a powerful ego, and the conviction that they control their own destinies is a central characteristic of their personalities. Facing up to the fact that they will not always be around to look after their business, or that a time will come when they will no longer be the best person to run the firm, is often too painful and threatening a concept for them to contemplate.

Reluctance to let go of control and power. The owner is accustomed to being in charge of the business and, more generally, is apt to be most comfortable in situations when he has total control. Also, many owners become entrepreneurs precisely because of a strong need to acquire and exercise power over others. It is not surprising, therefore, that surrendering authority can be seen to represent a huge sacrifice.

Loss of identity. Connected with the fear of losing power is the threat to the founder's personal identity posed by succession. As discussed in Chapter 2, the owner tends to identify very strongly with the firm, seeing it as an extension of himself and as a personal achievement that defines his place in the world. His sense of his own identity will be inextricably linked to his role in the business. The thought of letting go of the business can thus be experienced as a loss of personal effectiveness and potency, as well as a reawakening of old identity issues that may be hard to cope with at this late stage in the owner's life.

Bias against planning. Successful management transitions are generally the result of a major planning exercise that begins many years before the transition takes place. But, as highlighted elsewhere, owners tend to be 'doers' rather than planners. Their energies are usually focused on day-to-day operations, and their management style discourages formal planning, which they often perceive as bureaucratic and restrictive.

Inability to choose among children. In terms of business norms, the choice of a successor to lead and run the business should be based on competence. Family values, on the other hand, prescribe that children should not be the subject of an evaluation and selection process, but should be loved and treated equally. Family values tend to prevail in this conflict, with founders unwilling even to contemplate what they see as preferential treatment of one child at the expense of the others.

Fear of retirement. Many people feel threatened by the prospect of retirement, even those doing jobs that most of us assume they would be happy to leave. But owners of family firms are often, for all intents and purposes, in love with their business, and the thought of moving out of day-to-day work into the vacuum of retirement is seen as nothing short of a life-threatening event. The founder will probably have few outside interests that could be developed in retirement and, in the absence of such positive factors, will focus on negative considerations such as the anticipated loss of self-esteem and the risks of entrusting the business to an unproven successor.

Jealousy and rivalry. 'Nobody can run this business as well as me' is symptomatic of the exaggerated view many founders develop about their own importance when they have to struggle with succession. It also encapsulates the inevitable feelings of rivalry and jealousy that founders experience towards potential successors waiting to take over control of their beloved organisation. Usually, distrust concerning the successor's suitability and competence is the outward form in which these emotions manifest themselves. This factor can become even more serious when the successor is the founder's son. An extra dimension of fear and hostility is commonly introduced by the potential for father–son conflict.

The family
Forces operating against succession planning are not confined to those involving the founder. The family provide another source of pressures in favour of avoiding the issue.

The spouse's resistance to change. The founder's spouse is frequently reluctant to welcome and encourage her husband's move into retirement. She, too, may not relish the prospect of giving up the many key roles she has played in and around the family firm. As well as direct involvement in the business, the company will probably have become a centre of activity and a significant component of her social identity. She may fear that her importance will be diminished if her husband relinquishes control of the business.

Family taboos. The cultural norms that govern family behaviour discourage discussion between parents and children about the family's future after the parents die. This is particularly so in relation to financial matters, and an offspring who raises this would appear to be greedily interested in his inheritance rather than the health and longevity of his parents. Succession planning, of course, involves open discussion of precisely these topics and is thus usually avoided, even in the most well-adjusted families.

Other family factors that militate against planning and preparation for succession include the principle of equality among siblings, discussed earlier under 'The founder', and also the fear of parental death. The latter typically involves deep-rooted psychological worries about abandonment and separation, and such feelings can be too painful to permit participation in discussions about succession.

Employee and environmental factors
The firm's employees can present obstacles to succession, even though the prosperity and continuity of the business are in their best interests. For many employees, especially senior managers, their close personal relationship with the founder constitutes the most important advantage of working for the family firm. Replacement of the founder with a newcomer, seen as inexperienced and likely to make sweeping changes, is perceived by employees as a threat to their job satisfaction and security.

Outside the firm, important customers are also likely to prove resistant to change, reluctant to trust a new face. Similarly, the unwillingness of other entrepreneurs – the owner's peer group – to deal with their own succession acts to reinforce the founder's bias against planned management transition.

So founders have to face up to a minefield of complex and interrelated processes – psychological, emotional, individual, organisational and external – that are all operating against any kind of planned effort to manage the succession problem. It is hardly surprising, therefore, that so few family business founders are willing and able to organise effective succession planning, concentrating instead on coming up with one delaying tactic after another designed to put off the day when they will eventually have to grapple with the issue.

The all-important first step in managing the succession process involves recognising its importance and why it is so complex, and explaining these factors has been the objective so far in this chapter. A well-structured and systematic approach to counteracting all the negative forces is the next step, and we now examine some specific measures that founders can adopt to help them handle the planning of their succession.

SUCCESSFULLY MANAGING THE TRANSITION

Perhaps the central theme that recurs throughout this section is that the most successful transitions are those that result from establishing a partnership with the next generation, based on mutual responsibility, respect and commitment, rather than a unilateral decision by the owner to suddenly leave. The main elements in this partnership will be examined individually, but a summary is provided in Table 7.2.

Start planning early

Often the first real thoughts about succession are precipitated by the death or ill health of the MD. As well as the potential for serious damage to the business, this will be a time when the family is least able to give the matter adequate consideration. Insufficient planning for the death of the majority shareholder exposes the family to major cash flow problems in the form of inheritance tax liabilities but no liquid assets with which to settle them. In other cases, the succession proceeds in an atmosphere of mutual acrimony and guilt as family members, unable to understand or control the process they are caught up in, look for somewhere to place the blame.

At one company, for example, the founder had made no

Table 7.2   *A succession checklist*

- Start planning early
- Encourage inter-generational
  teamwork
- Develop a written succession plan
- Involve the family and colleagues in
  your thinking
- Take advantage of outside help
- Establish a training process
- Plan for retirement
- Make retirement timely and
  unequivocal

---

concrete plans for succession (although he had made provision against estate duties). The sons (who had left school aged 16) had become increasingly involved in the business, albeit it in a fairly haphazard fashion. Then one day, after an argument with his son over a business decision, the founder declared himself fed up with running the company, and walked out leaving his sons to run things on their own. This left the firm in a state of considerable chaos for some time after, was the source of much family friction, and left the brothers feeling ill-equipped to manage the enterprise they found themselves controlling.

Succession should not be *an event*, but a carefully planned process that takes place over time. Ideally, the owner's transition from MD to chairman of the board or full retirement is so gradual as to be imperceptible. Successors grow into their roles, earning the respect and confidence of the owner, and the owner gradually becomes accustomed to a new role, rather than being abruptly replaced in the position of authority.

Developing a full understanding of the transition process and its effect upon family members is critical, and this also takes a long time. The various options need to be assessed, the family must be given adequate opportunity to reflect upon the implications of decisions, and a gradual succession timetable needs to be structured and agreed.

Encourage inter-generational teamwork

This is really an additional perspective on starting to plan early. It is all very well for founders to say they want the next generation to take over, but it's vital to establish and foster inter-generational teamwork if the build up to the transition, the transition itself, and what happens afterwards are to be as trouble-free as possible.

As discussed in Chapter 1, family businesses tend to become more complex with the passing of time, and especially with the transition from one generation to the next. With succeeding generations, the intensity of emotional factors that surround the family's involvement in the business increases. Items of 'emotional baggage' (unresolved issues left over from the previous generation) do not disappear – they loom ever larger. If, for example, one brother feels he has been 'done down' by another brother, and this grievance is not settled before the brothers die, then when the next generation succeeds the grudge will live on and fester. Similarly, if a father hasn't chosen between two children because he doesn't want to upset anybody, then after he has left the scene they will fight it out between them and try to resolve a critical issue that ought to have been sorted out by the father when he was around. Establishing inter-generational teamwork implies the generations recognising these sorts or problems, talking about them, and trying to find solutions. Assuming such issues will just be forgotten about over time is a fundamental mistake – they always come back later on, by which time they are generally more complicated and more difficult to resolve.

Another inter-generational issue involves appreciating the importance of financial independence between generations and trying to make provision for this in the succession plan. Too often cases arise where a founder, for example, is imposing a sort of emotional blackmail on his successors: although formally retired, he may well be drawing a large company pension, and any advice he has for the new generation could be, or could be seen to be, 'loaded' because of a vested interest in ensuring his pension income is safeguarded.

One way of achieving financial (and a measure of psychological) independence between generations is through what's called an 'inter-generational loan'. In order to buy out the departing generation and to ensure that it ceases to have any financial claims on the company, the new generation takes out a loan, secured on the assets of the business. This will usually involve the purchase of shares, so legal advice must be obtained to make sure that the transaction is constructed in such a way that the company does not fall foul of the general prohibition on companies giving any kind of financial assistance (including security) for the purchase of their own shares. Provided the necessary clearances are obtained, the banks are now much more willing to provide inter-generational loans. As a result, there has been a significant increase in such transactions in recent years, especially for third generation family firms (more buy-outs occur in the third generation than at any other time). However, securing inter-generational financial independence and freedom of action for the incoming leadership team should be regarded as a vital ingredient of all succession plans, regardless of which generations are involved.

Develop a written succession plan

A written plan that incorporates a step-by-step approach to dealing with all the practical and psychological aspects of the transition process will prove immensely valuable. The thought required to formulate and write down the stages of the process will be useful in itself, and the existence of a formal document that everybody is aware of, and has been consulted about, will significantly reduce the potential for doubts and misunderstandings.

The plan should include the detailed timetable that plots each phase of both the founder's reduced participation in the business, as well as the training and mentoring programme attaching to the successor's expanding role and responsibilities.

But the plan should not be confined to issues surrounding the top job. The structure of the management team in the next generation – what individuals will be in it, how it will operate, and so on – is also an important ingredient in the planning process.

When the plan is complete, communicate it (or at least its principal conclusions) to your family, your employees, and to outsiders who have an interest in the continuity and success of the business, such as your bank manager, customers and suppliers. Tangible evidence of your serious approach to the problems of succession will impress and reassure them and, at the same time, will give everyone the opportunity to plan for a smooth transition.

Involve everyone and obtain outside help

It is a good idea to appoint a succession working party, consisting of the owner, selected family members and key trusted employees. The group is responsible for developing the succession plan and monitoring its implementation. The latter is important in ensuring that the plan is accomplishing the desired organisational results, including generating individual psychological responses that will be required to sustain the transition.

It is the founder's responsibility to initiate and lead the succession planning process, but the task force gives everyone most directly concerned an opportunity to discuss their thoughts and fears openly. By providing a forum for debate, it should help to reduce negative emotional reaction within the family.

While input from the family and employees about their concerns, interests and priorities is very important, the fact is that only the founder fully understands the complex emotional and managerial issues associated with succession planning. Because of this, founders should try to involve as many people as possible in the process – anyone, in fact, who may be able to offer useful advice and support during this critical phase. For example:

- A strong, independent board of directors can provide an invaluable source of expertise and objectivity during succession planning.
- Family business consultants are often skilled in dealing with these issues.
- Your accountant and your solicitor will probably have considerable experience of succession and may be able to provide new insights.
- Peer groups, comprising business colleagues who are themselves facing, or who have already been through the succession transition will almost certainly be helpful. Sharing and comparing experiences can serve as a much-needed source of ideas, strategies and support.

So consult with people who can provide you with guidance, but at the same time it is vital not to lose sight of the fact that succession planning requires decisions affecting not only the business, but also your family, your own retirement, how you are to spend your time, and so on – in other words, 'life decisions' that you will be called upon to make only once in your career. It makes sense to seek out advice, but in the final analysis the decisions are yours, by right.

Develop a training process
Many owners assume that their children will want to enter the family business, or they put pressure on them to do so.

While the children are growing up, it is important to try and keep an open mind about this possibility, and to remember that their perception of the business is being formed mainly on the basis of what you tell them about it. If you are always complaining about the problems of running the firm it is not unlikely that they will shy away from the prospect and elect to choose other careers. But, similarly, if your children are conditioned from birth to believe that the business represents a golden inheritance and that perpetuating it is their destiny, then they will tend to view joining the firm either as a lifetime meal ticket, or as a weighty obligation rather than an opportunity. Entirely insulating the children from the business should also be avoided because you may be conveying an unintended message that they should pursue careers elsewhere.

It is not easy, but try to find a balance that enables the children to share your dream, while making sure you do not put excessive pressure on them to feel that they have no choice but to be part of it. Tell them about the exciting and challenging aspects of running the business as well as the negative considerations. Let them get first-hand experience of the firm, perhaps working in it during summer holidays, but always balance your enthusiasm by making it clear that you will understand and be supportive should they choose other careers. At the end of the day, their decision to join should be freely made and based on a thorough understanding of the privileges and responsibilities that come with the job, and an acceptance of the hard work and commitment required. Inadequate preparation and training, or undue pressure, condemns many innocent children to unhappy careers that are neither satisfying for them nor productive for the business.

After school
Once the children have completed their education, encourage them to obtain extended work experience in another organisation, preferably in your industry, before joining the family company. The most successful non-first generation managers of family firms have often spent much of their early working life outside the family business. They gain wider perspectives and experience, and competing in the outside world allows them to achieve a sense of independence and self-esteem that affords a much sounder foundation on which they can decide whether they really want to enter the family firm. If they do join, the outside work experience is likely to help them do their job better, and will make it easier for them to gain the support and respect of non-family employees. If they do not join, it is their choice, they will have the comfort of knowing they can compete elsewhere for a job, and you should be happy that they have found a path through to satisfying careers.

In-house training

The typical route to the top for the heir apparent in many traditional family firms involves a series of jobs within the firm, often beginning with mastering the workings of the electric kettle. While learning every job on the way up can have a value in particular businesses, some observers take the view that the development of managerial talent is a long process and that time is too short to waste it on direct experience of even the most menial tasks simply for its own sake. Whether starting at the bottom really adds much boils down to a question of preference but, overall, the important point is to make sure that all training is worthwhile and appropriate in relation to the end-result you are seeking to achieve.

Also, be aware that because of the emotional involvement, fathers can be very bad teachers. Help your child to find a mentor, other than yourself, within the organisation so that his or her performance will not be coloured by the family connection. It is no good trying to train your children to be duplicates of you. For better or worse, they grew up in a different environment, probably had different educational backgrounds, have different aspirations, and are entering a business that is quite different from when you founded or entered it. This does not mean that you give them a free hand to take over the business that has taken you a lifetime to build, but it does mean that in providing advice and sharing your experience, you help them to grow according to their own abilities and in their own way. What is called for is patience on the part of both teacher and pupil, and a commitment by both to making the training process work.

It is worth summarising here some of the key conclusions from Chapter 6 that are especially relevant following the children's entry to the business:

- *Define their roles.* Conflict over children's functions in the business can be a major source of tension. Consider separating responsibilities, either on the basis of operational criteria (e.g. production and marketing) or, if the business lends itself to it, geographically. Establish

the responsibilities of each role in writing and provide
procedures on how overlaps will be handled.

- *Set objectives and provide feedback.* Employees, *including
children*, need to know what is expected in their jobs.
They also need regular feedback about their
performance, including recognition for achievements and
constructive advice on aspects of their work that need
improving.
- *Pay children the going rate.* Many owners pay their
children either far below or far above their true worth.
But experience has shown that the fairest and healthiest
remuneration system is to pay family members the
market rate for their jobs, as though they were working
for another firm. Other, less objective systems often lead
to resentment and conflict.

Make your retirement timely and unequivocal

Unfortunately, founders do not always know when to step down.
Succession is much more likely to proceed smoothly if the
founder's retirement takes place at a time when he is still in full
command of his abilities and able to provide guidance to senior
managers when they seek it. Life-cycle analysts have
highlighted the difficulties that can occur when founders hold
on to their positions beyond about age 65. They tend to become
'out of phase' with their successors who themselves are likely to
be in their late-30s or 40s and impatient for independence,
recognition and opportunities for leadership.

In addition, having set a definite date for leaving, the founder
should stick to it. A public commitment in the form of a precise
timetable for the founder's departure included in a written
succession plan will help to reduce the possibilities for confusion
or delay. This does not mean that the founder must cease to play
any role in the business, but it does mean that his new role has
been well defined and does not include participation in
day-to-day aspects of the business. 'Semi-retirement', where all
important decisions continue to require the former MD's
clearance (albeit via the newly installed fax machine in his

'retirement home') simply indicates that the succession issue remains unresolved.

Plan for retirement

It is important to prepare yourself emotionally and financially for a new phase of your life that does not revolve exclusively around the family business.

Financial preparations are discussed in detail in Chapters 9 and 10. At the emotional level, experts are more or less unanimous that this phase is most likely to be successfully negotiated if you are retiring *to* a new life of interesting activities, rather than from your old one, which implies that your useful and productive days are over. Think, therefore, about how best to use your new-found leisure time, and also plan your future work activities. Many people these days set out on a second career once they have retired from their first.

Do not, however, overlook the fact that founders remain a vital resource to the family firm, even though they have passed on day-to-day operational responsibility to their successors. Many founders, as part of their succession plan, assume new, productive roles in the company, taking on, for example, long-term strategic planning, new product development, or expansion into international markets. The founder can also play a vital role in fostering management continuity, connecting the new managers with individuals and organisations that may be critically important to the future success and prosperity of the company.

CHOOSING A SUCCESSOR

Family business owners should resist the temptation to favour succession candidates just because they are in their own image and likeness. As discussed earlier in this chapter, viewing succession as a cloning process is likely to prove a mistake.

In evaluating candidates, important questions need to be asked:

- Are they committed to the company's mission?
- Do they have the ability to move the organisation forward?
- Can they think independently and exercise good judgement?
- Do they have the leadership and inter-personal talents required to motivate others?

A much more fundamental point, however, is whether the founder is the right person to be asking these questions, conducting the evaluation process, and eventually choosing a successor. A number of experts have concluded that no MD should be responsible for the selection of his own successor. Harry Levinson summarises the argument well:

> Each of us in his own unconscious way seeks omnipotence and immortality. To varying degrees, each wants his achievements to stand as an enduring monument to himself; each wants to demonstrate that he was necessary to his organisation, that it cannot do without him. This pressure is particularly strong for entrepreneurs and those who hold their positions for long periods of time. As a result, although executives consciously seek to perpetuate their organisations through the wise choice of successors, unconsciously they also seek to demonstrate that no one can succeed them.[3]

To avoid these dangers, the advice and assistance of a strong board of directors is invaluable, both in assessing the capabilities of family members in the business and in making the final decision. In particular, an experienced and

---

[3]Reprinted by permission of the *Harvard Business Review*. Excerpt from 'Don't choose your own successor' written by Harry Levinson (November–December, 1971). Copyright © 1971 by the President and Fellows of Harvard College; all rights reserved.

independent non-executive director may be able to offer a perspective free of the processes in which the MD and other members of the firm and family are caught up. Outside professional advisers can also be consulted as an extra source of objectivity.

Who to choose?
Regardless of whether the founder decides who is to succeed him, or responsibility for the decision is passed to third parties, a number of important considerations relating to succession candidates from within the family need to be borne in mind.

The 'logical' successor
Sometimes the choice is straightforward. There may be a single successor who is both capable and committed and who, during the succession-planning process, grows naturally into the role. But some families define 'logical' to mean that the eldest son is automatically the first choice. While this eliminates uncertainty and reduces the likelihood of rivalry among the children, the clear disadvantage of such a rule is that it may lead to the appointment of a leader who is less qualified than other candidates.

Choosing from among 'equals'
It was emphasised in Chapter 5 that family members should be recruited into the firm only if, on business grounds, they possess the skills needed to carry out the job effectively. Exactly the same principle should apply to the recruitment of a new MD, even if this offends the family norm that all children must be treated equally.

There are cases, however, where family businesses actually find themselves without a leader because the owner was unable, or unwilling, to face up to the difficult decision of choosing a successor from among his children. Others sometimes seek a marginally better, but still ill-conceived compromise involving the rotation of management responsibility among the children. By the time that one gets to grips with this difficult and central job, their term ends and it is the turn of another of the children to take over.

A further group tries shared management under which there is no 'boss' in the accepted sense, but a partnership among the owners with decisions taken jointly. There are circumstances in which this can work, especially where the business readily divides into clearly defined and largely autonomous segments, but it requires a high degree of trust and harmony among the owners. It helps if they are of relatively equal abilities and possess an unusually strong willingness to compromise and to accept consensus decision making. Even then, the owners should agree on a method of resolving deadlock, perhaps involving the services of a respected third party owning a minority stake that can be voted to break stalemate situations.

Shared management is most likely to be successful when there is a limited number of owners. Instances of enduring success, however, are rare and do not threaten the general rule that most businesses need a single leader who is the ultimate authority.

Do not overlook daughters

Daughters often possess unique qualifications for the MD's job, and their increasing importance within family businesses was discussed in detail in Chapter 2. In particular, the absence of the potentially troublesome father–son relationship is often cited by owners of family businesses in which a daughter's rise to power has come as something of a surprise.

In-laws as successors

The unique issues surrounding in-laws as successors were also examined in Chapter 2. The involvement of committed sons-in-law or daughters-in-law often provides next-generation leadership and brings new dimensions of strength to the family business. But the increasing incidence of marriage breakdown in Ireland can have a severe impact when it involves an in-law who is in a key management position.

Some families are able to separate the family and business

considerations, and the in-law continues to work in the business. Others find this untenable and the in-law has to leave. (Often the family insists on, and provides for, an immediate buy-back of the firm's shares held by the in-law and the family member in the event of marriage breakdown.) Ultimately, the risks of a potential marriage breakdown have to be weighed against the benefits an in-law can bring to the business, and there are no easy answers.

More than one family unit
Succession from the second generation onwards generally involves more than one family unit. Usually, the number of potential successors is larger, and the choices become more difficult. As participation in the business grows, so too does the potential for conflict, particularly when share ownership is equal between the family units. Hiring professional managers to run the business (considered in the next section) provides a clear solution to the co-ownership problem. But if the families want to remain actively involved in the business the owners need to develop strict policies to govern its future management.

And if there is no qualified successor?
Although you may have a huge amount of emotional capital invested in the business, and wish to see it continued by your children, it may be self-defeating to force a family management transition if the right circumstances do not exist. Perhaps none of the children has the ability needed to run a business, or maybe rivalry between them is so extreme that none would accept one of the others as leader.

If you make an honest assessment of the situation and conclude that there is little chance of a successful management transition to the next generation, you should begin to look for some alternatives.

Dividing the business
If sibling rivalry effectively precludes the children proceeding together, it may be worth considering a division of the company.

Assuming the business is suited to such a demerger, the children can each take over different parts, which then develop independently.

Selling the company

When a transition within the family is not achievable, you may be better off selling the business rather than forcing the succession issue. The decision to sell is likely to be traumatic and, compared with a transfer of the firm to the next generation, there may be some adverse tax consequences (although these can be minimised with careful planning).

It is important to try and disentangle the emotional considerations from the financial ones. A useful approach is to ask a business owner who has ruled out the possibility of a sale, 'What if I was to hand over to you now a cheque for IR£3 million representing the value of the business? Would you put the money into property, or the stock market, or a building society – or would you buy a business like yours?' The response to the last possibility is usually, 'No'. The question is rarely posed in such stark terms, but it should be. A sale may be the best option in order to preserve the owner's financial security and harmony in the family. Selling is looked at in detail in Chapter 9.

Appointing non-family managers

Many families decide to hire outside professional managers if it is not feasible for a family member to take over. The major issue here is one of trust – will the family's principal store of wealth be safe in the hands of an outsider? On the other hand, family members in the business, aware of the problems they would have in filling the role, often prefer reporting to a respected professional manager.

The appointment of outside managers becomes a particularly relevant consideration once the family business reaches the third generation and beyond. By this stage there can be dozens of family members with a stake in the firm, and introducing professional management often represents the only realistic solution to the succession issue.

Sometimes families try to avoid having to resort to outsider managers by appointing as MD someone who has worked for the family for years, and is seen as part of it. This can be disastrous. Such a manager will have had little opportunity to develop an individual style, and is frequently under considerable pressure from the family to adopt a role of stewardship rather than leadership.

Employing a 'bridge'

If the obstacles to family succession are temporary (for example, when the children are too young or inexperienced to take over from the founder), a caretaker MD can be appointed to run the firm until the transition within the family eventually takes place. Referred to as a 'bridge', the individual is usually a talented professional manager. He will expect to be well paid to compensate for the short-term and essential nature of his task. It is not uncommon for such a caretaker also to act as a mentor to the succeeding generation. The children may find it easier to take advice from him rather than from their father, and the bridge takes on the role of grooming them for the future.

Succession management: Key suggestions

- Founders need a well-structured and systematic approach to succession planning if they are to overcome all the forces that favour doing nothing.
- Start planning early, involve the family and colleagues, and take advantage of outside help.
- Let your children know that you will welcome them into the business if this is their choice. Equally, however, make clear that you will understand and be supportive if they choose other careers.

Key suggestions (contd.)

- If the children do want to join, encourage them to obtain extended work experience in another organisation first.
- Once they join, provide them with a training programme that is relevant and worthwhile, that allows them to make mistakes and to achieve their highest level of potential.
- Choose your successor as soon as you can and, also as early as possible, establish a target date for your retirement. This should be far enough ahead so that your successor and everyone else can plan and prepare for it. Once you have set a definite date, stick to it.

---

8 The Children's Perspective

This chapter is directed to children in family businesses. As well as examining the preparation and training required for those who are to take over leadership of the firm, it also looks at the role of other family managers and family employees. All family members usually feel under intense pressure to prove their worth – to themselves, to non-family employees, to outsiders – and, most of all, to prove to the founder that they are capable of building the business and continuing the vision.

The chapter covers how children should go about deciding whether or not they want to join the firm, the best ways of preparing for entry, and how they should handle their relationships with non-family employees as well as with the owner. Some practical suggestions are also included on preparing for succession, and how children in a family business can help the owner through the transition process.

TO JOIN OR NOT TO JOIN?

Succession between generations in family businesses is less straightforward than it used to be. Today's generation is growing up in a commercial culture that is radically different from that in which earlier family members took on responsibility. Increasingly well educated, cosmopolitan and independent, they are less willing to be viewed as the automatic heir apparent. Furthermore, in recent years businesses have come to be seen more as disposable commodities – to be started up, grown, and then sold – and young people find it less easy to identify with the idea of the family business as a sacred trust for future generations. The advantages and disadvantages of joining the family firm are therefore being weighed much more carefully.

In starting up a business, the first two or three years are often the most difficult as the entrepreneur, under-capitalised and afraid of failure, struggles to establish the firm. Many young people with entrepreneurial aspirations, who have grown up in a family business, find it more attractive to avoid the problems and pain of this phase and, instead, enter the already established family firm. Others, however, see joining the firm as a 'no win' option – if they succeed, people will say 'Well why not, he started after all the hard work had been done', while if they fail, they have squandered a golden opportunity and destroyed a family legacy. A range of other worries about working in the business need to be faced, including:

- Will it be possible for me to live up to the founder's expectations?
- Will I be able to establish my own independence and freedom to act, or will I always be operating in the founder's shadow?
- How will I get along with the founder when we have to work closely together everyday?
- Can I establish working relationships with my brothers and sisters, or will there be too much arguing and conflict?
- Will the employees respect me?

Weighing up the pros and cons
Children in a family business have a unique opportunity to build a challenging and enriching career for themselves.

The advantages of their situation are obvious. The business is already up and running. It offers job security and probably an attractive remuneration package. Working in a family business can be extremely rewarding. These businesses often possess a unique atmosphere that encourages a 'sense of belonging', there is extra commitment to a common purpose, they are stable and reliable, and they can take decisions very quickly, all of which contribute enormously to the firm's success potential, providing it with a valuable edge on its competitors. Also, from a personal standpoint, family members enjoy a special status both inside and outside the firm, and it is a distinct possibility that one day they may become owners of the business.

Nevertheless, there is a price that has to be paid for all these advantages. Family businesses are usually not diversified multinationals that can withstand downturns in some of their markets relatively easily. There must always be a doubt about whether the business will survive in the long term, and if you are looking for this type of career security then the family business may not be right for you. If you join for the wrong reasons (searching for a safe haven, for example), or because you have not thought through the emotional complexities of family business life and the commitment you must be prepared to make, then it is likely to be a decision you will always regret.

It is important to try to plan your career with the founder, discussing his ambitions for the firm and how he sees his own timetable for the future. If you are unsure about what to do, endeavour to get his support for you to try other alternatives. Acquiring some outside business experience beforehand is almost always a good idea, and consider entering on a trial basis as another possibility. It is better to have this sort of discussion very early on before you have invested several years of your life, and before the founder has invested time and effort in your training. Remember also that the founder may have been building up his hopes and expectations for many years that you will join the firm, eventually take over, and continue the dream. If the family business really is not for you, it is much better if this possibility is talked about openly at an early stage in order to limit the founder's disappointment, and to give him time to plan other options.

On the other hand, there is evidence that founders today are less apt to count on their children as automatic successors. There is growing concern about the long-term welfare of the business in circumstances where successors have grown up believing that they will inherit the shares as a matter of right, rather than having to tangibly demonstrate their level of commitment. One solution to this concern involves the children being given some shares, but only on condition that they purchase the balance of their eventual holding. The need to find, say, IR£50,000 for 35 per cent of the company as a condition for receiving the remaining 65 per cent free, could become an increasingly common requirement that will obviously help children to decide just how serious their commitment and desire to join the family firm really is.

THE IMPORTANCE OF OUTSIDE EXPERIENCE

In advising family businesses, so much depends on the unique history and idiosyncrasies of individual firms that universal truths are in short supply. So, on the rare occasions they do crop up they deserve to be highlighted. *A golden rule is that before entering the family business, children should take some time to work and to prove themselves in the outside world.* There are various reasons for this.

Self-esteem and confidence
Succeeding at something on your own, away from the family nest, will help to build your self-esteem and the confidence you have in your own abilities. If you decide to join the family firm, the experience will give you an extra perspective on your role, helping you to establish your own identity and to succeed on your own merits. And if, on the other hand, you choose to leave the firm at some stage, you will have the comfort of knowing you have already proved that you can compete and win through in a world in which the required qualifications extend beyond having the right surname.

This outside experience need not be confined to working in

another organisation (although this does offer particular benefits that will be discussed later). You should also consider acquiring general business qualifications – perhaps enroling for a business studies course or an MBA. Nowadays there is no shortage of such courses to choose from, ranging from full-time residential studies, or two-week intensive sandwich courses spread at intervals over a year, through to evening classes that can be combined with a day job.

Wider business experience

Learning how other firms work will almost certainly benefit you throughout your business career.

Try to find a larger, more professionally managed company than your family's, and preferably, although not necessarily, in the same industry. Moving straight from full-time education into the family business can only tend to increase its natural potential to become introverted, whereas your outside experience is likely to generate a fund of ideas to bring back to the family firm, helping you to make it more extrovert and flexible.

This might include, for instance, new production or marketing methods, as well as administrative or strategic planning techniques that will assist in professionalising the business more quickly and more effectively. There is a lot to be said for learning management skills in an objective atmosphere outside the family company.

In an example taken from a recent newspaper article, a family firm which had seemingly lost its way was rescued as a result of the efforts of a new managing director. The son of his predecessor, he had not intended to enter the family business. The sudden and unexpected death of his father and the request of other family members changed his mind and he returned from overseas to take control. His substantial work experience outside the family firm enabled the new MD to recognise quickly the need for change. He was able to transform the company from an introvert to an extrovert organisation, and to ensure its survival.

Credibility with non-family employees

A founder's son or daughter who leaves school or university and straight away becomes deputy managing director of the family business is likely to be the cause of enormous resentment among non-family employees. This can manifest itself as resentment not only against the individual concerned but also against the whole family. Feeling often runs so high in this type of situation that you find key non-family managers simply walking out and placing the survival of the business in jeopardy.

Your credibility will be enhanced when you enter the business with some experience under your belt. The fact that you will need to earn employee respect rather than having it freely given is discussed later. You will have taken quite a few steps along this path if, when you enter the family firm, the employees know that on your own initiative you went out and joined another organisation, gaining first-hand experience of the real world of work.

Peter Davis of Wharton Business School tells an interesting story of how, at the start of each academic year, he explains the fundamental importance of outside experience to his new undergraduate class of young people from family businesses. Throughout the course, he emphasises the point and discusses all the advantages summarised here, and then, at the end of the semester says, 'OK, of you 25 students, how many of you now are going to get some experience outside before joining the family business' – and usually about three hands go up. Davis then asks, 'What happened to the other 22 – were you not listening', and the response comes back, 'You don't understand Professor, I'm a special case.' So most people tend to feel that their situation is special, and that they have uniquely important reasons for entering the firm straight away. If you find yourself thinking this, it is well worth thinking again.

WORKING IN THE BUSINESS

It is important to plan the progress of your training and education within the business. For the first few years, your main objective will be to learn as much as possible about it as you can. Develop a structured plan with the founder, and try to allocate a period for every important department so as to pick up a thorough grounding, as well as helping you to decide which parts of the operation are of most interest to you.

Time spent on manual and repetitive jobs just for the sake of doing everything is usually not very productive. Try to ensure that jobs you take on are a progression from what you did last, and that they represent a meaningful learning experience in the context of your plan. It is difficult to be specific about this because much depends on the nature and size of the business. For example, a child joining a mail order business will not necessarily gain much from time spent operating the firm's computer systems. But in a software company this will clearly form a central element in the training process.

As well as learning about specific tasks, take a broader view of the company and the industry in which it operates. What is the firm's mission and how well is it doing in achieving these core objectives? What plan does it have for the next three to five years? What are its main strengths and weaknesses? How is the firm positioned within its industry? Who are its principal competitors? Is the industry expanding or shrinking, and where will it be in five years' time? Arrange to become a member of your industry trade organisation and keep up to date with all the latest publications about the sector, as well as the leading studies on business management.

Here are some other guidelines on working in the business.

Seek out a mentor. Most people will be willing to help if you ask them, but go further than this and try to establish a special relationship with a non-family mentor figure within the organisation. A key manager who has been with the firm for a long time and who knows the business inside out, will often be available to take on this dual role of teacher and friend. Such a relationship can operate largely free from all the emotional aspects of your family connection, and is potentially extremely valuable.

Work at establishing your own identity.   Everyone working in, and doing business with the firm will know that you are the MD's son or daughter. So you will have to make special efforts to establish yourself as an independent personality, prepared to succeed or fail on your own merits. Discuss the problem with the founder so he understands the possible difficulties, and make sure that he goes out of his way to treat you like any other employee. You do not want extra favours or privileges that mark you out and serve as a constant reminder to everyone of your special position.

Gain the respect of employees.   When you first join the family business, your credibility with non-family employees will probably be minimal. They know why you got the job, and they are likely to be watching you closely, and with a degree of scepticism. Some of them may even perceive you as a threat to the long-established and familiar ways of the business, and will

"ITS A PORTABLE PHONE SON...DON'T WORRY, SIMPSON'LL CARRY IT FOR YOU."

try to subvert you. Acceptance as a leader will certainly not flow from your surname and will have to be earned.

Already having some outside work experience when you arrive will help a lot, but you will still have to prove your merit. Avoid seeking special privileges, be prepared to listen to people and, most of all, show yourself keen to learn and willing to work hard.

Tread carefully. You will bring a fresh viewpoint to the business, and one of your main contributions may be to question the effectiveness of its operational procedures and systems. You may feel that it resembles an historical monolith and that there is a real need for professionalisation – but go carefully. Learn how the existing methods work and how they evolved before you try to change them. Both the founder and the employees are likely to be wary about altering systems that work, and there is bound to be resistance to the bright newcomer who wants to change everything around. Try not to make the issue into a crusade. Instead, be patient, build up your credibility, and take a step-by-step approach. Your objectivity, unencumbered by the weight of tradition, may play an important role in helping to position the company for future growth.

Beware of sibling rivalry. If you have brothers or sisters who are also working in the business, remember that some rivalry is normal and bound to occur, but try to prevent these feelings developing into a destructive force. This requires a determination to manage sibling rivalry rather than being managed by it, and it also requires a willingness to sometimes subordinate personal issues to the best interests of the business. Try to agree on a code of behaviour that recognises that the welfare of the business is paramount, and that establishes procedures for the resolution of differences.

Prepare for succession. Your role in the challenging process of management succession centres on being thoroughly prepared, as well as doing everything you can to ensure that the transition takes place in as smooth a way as possible. In learning about every facet of the business, you will need to demonstrate a level of ability and commitment that will earn you the respect of the founder and the employees, as well as the firm's customers and suppliers. The ideal result will be that you gradually take on more and more responsibility so that assuming leadership, when the time comes, represents a natural and trouble-free progression, not an abrupt change.

If, instead of you, another family member or an outsider is chosen to be the next MD, you must either provide the successor with your full and unequivocal support, or be prepared to seek other career opportunities outside the family firm.

YOUR RELATIONSHIP WITH THE FOUNDER

It is important not to overemphasise the problems and conflicts that can arise in relationships between founders and their children. If you enjoy your father's company, and your temperament, motivation and expectations are in harmony with his, you can enjoy an outstandingly close and productive business life together. But, at the other extreme, the fact remains that if you do not share a compatible outlook and there is excessive conflict, then working together can become a nightmare for you both.

Resolving your differences

When conflict is a problem, however serious, it is important to realise that most entrepreneurial fathers seem unable to resolve the dilemmas raised on their own. Apart from the age difference, they tend to be rigid in outlook and find it difficult to understand that when faced with an alternative, equally valid point of view, it is possible for them to accept it without appearing to be weak. A lot of the responsibility for finding solutions will therefore fall on your shoulders, and you will need a mature and patient approach. Remember that your father's and your own perspectives on life in general, and the business in particular, are liable to be inherently different:

- Your father belongs to a different generation. He probably will not have received as good an education as you, and his values and fears are likely to be difficult for you to grasp – and vice versa.
- You may feel that the organisational structure of the business has been outgrown. Your father, on the other hand, may see little reason to change methods that have proved effective, or he may see change as threatening his ability to keep control, as well as limiting his creativity and flexibility.
- You have joined an established business and you may identify opportunities for growth if the firm is prepared to increase its risk exposure in a controlled and limited way – moving into new product areas, for example, or taking on some debt. But at a later stage in life, and having risked everything in the early days, your father's priorities are more likely to centre on conserving the business and protecting his financial security.
- You will probably view your father's approaching retirement as his just reward for a life of hard work and achievement in successfully building the business. The time is coming for him to take things easy and to pass on the burden to you. Your father's perspective may be quite different. For many years, the business has probably been his consuming interest, and he may well see retirement as a loss of authority, status and self-esteem.

Your appreciation of the existence and scope of these different perspectives should help you to understand when and how they are likely to lead to friction. It should also help you to develop strategies, based on patience and diplomacy, that minimise their potential for conflict.

Your role in the retirement process

As an illustration of such a strategy, let's look at one of the examples of conflicting outlooks – the founder's retirement. Here are a few ideas:

1. If your relations with your father have centred mainly around the business, try to cultivate your personal ties by getting to know him better: spend more time together, take an interest in his interests, and so on.
2. Try to understand what retirement means for your father. Encourage him to talk about his hopes and fears.
3. Help him to draw up and implement a detailed succession plan along the lines discussed in Chapter 7.
4. Be sympathetic, and work with him at directly addressing the main concerns. Openly acknowledge the importance of his achievements.
5. If he is worried that his usefulness will end when he steps down, make it clear that you will still need his support and guidance, and the benefit of his experience.
6. Look at ways he might continue to be involved with the business after retirement, even though operational responsibilities will have passed to you. Possibilities include becoming chairman of the board, taking on the role of company adviser and mentor, or perhaps using his skills to start a new venture for the firm.

A coherent strategy like this, based on communication and a shared understanding of the issues, provides the common ground on which you can preserve a constructive relationship with your father, as well as helping him to overcome the main emotional difficulties of the succession process.

The children's perspective: Key suggestions

- Before you join the family business, discuss the prospect as well as other career possibilities with the founder.
- If you do join, make sure it is because you are committed, not because it is expected of you or an easy option.

Key suggestions (contd.)

- Obtain outside work experience first. It will help you to develop an objective view of your own talents and abilities, and will also make you more effective if you do join.
- Once you start work in the family firm, establish a planned training programme encompassing all aspects of the business.
- Show that you are willing to work hard and provide an extra dimension of commitment.
- Earn the respect of employees through your behaviour and dedication, and reject special privileges.
- In relation to succession, talk to your father about his concerns, and help him to prepare a succession plan.

9 Relinquishing Control

Financial security is important to a successful retirement for the family business owner. A statement of the obvious perhaps, but many owners in fact neglect their personal finances.

Even very basic personal financial planning involves a bewildering array of increasingly sophisticated products and strategies. For business owners, the choices are especially complex, and few are willing or able to devote enough time to planning their financial future properly. Also, people who own successful enterprises often tend to believe that the business itself represents their personal nest-egg – that it will, in some unspecified way, guarantee them financial security when the time comes for them to step down. This may well turn out to be true, but it involves a number of assumptions that cannot always be taken for granted.

Sometimes the way ahead is clear and uncomplicated. If you have enough money invested outside the business to provide for a secure retirement, and you have planned for management succession, you may want to pass on your shares in the family firm to the next generation. The best ways to accomplish this will be discussed in Chapter 10.

On the other hand, you may have no suitable successor, or you may feel that family relationships are likely to improve if the business is taken out of the equation. Perhaps you have simply had enough of the business and would like to take on a new challenge. The answer in such circumstances may be to sell the

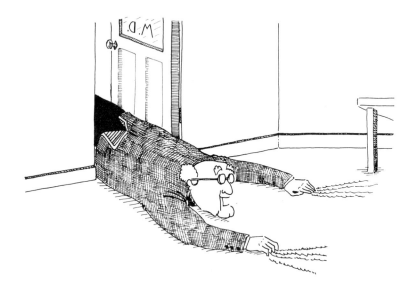

"OF COURSE, I COULD ALWAYS STAY ON... IN A PURELY ADVISORY CAPACITY..."

company. One owner, after refereeing the latest in a long series of squabbles between his children, said, 'Sell the company? Hell's bells, I wish I could sell the family!'

In this chapter, therefore, the aim is to explore ways of providing for the owner's financial security during retirement, as well as how to sell the business if that is what he wants to do. Taxation is a critical consideration affecting both areas and, while it is possible here to give broad indications of the current tax consequences of different courses of action, it is not practical to present a detailed analysis. Irish taxation laws, regulations, and interpretations are complex and constantly changing, and you should consult a competent tax adviser before deciding to pursue any of the options discussed.

Finally, the chapter also covers the important topic of share purchase agreements that enable the buy-out of family shareholders. Such mechanisms can be crucial in resolving the complications of multiple family ownership which tend to arise when family firms reach the third generation and beyond.

BUILDING FINANCIAL SECURITY

If you have owned the family business for a long time, you may well have become accustomed to a substantial salary, along with a package of valuable benefits such as a company car, private medical insurance, and so on. But if you continue to own the business after retirement, this financial situation is likely to alter abruptly. The amount of money you can draw from the business will be limited by its capacity to pay a salary to both yourself and your successor as MD, and by rules that limit tax deductibility.

Also, if most of your assets are tied up in the company (as is the case for many family business owners), your retirement income will become dependent on the ability of the next generation to manage the business successfully. This may not be a problem, but some owners are actually forced out of retirement to take over from incompetent children in order to protect their own financial security.

Money into or out of the business?

Financial peace of mind is a crucial ingredient in a successful retirement, but there are two schools of thought on the best way for business owners to engineer this security. Broadly, they can either operate a policy of continuously taking money out of the business during their period of tenure, or they can leave this money in the balance sheet so that it builds up to the point when, on retirement, a restructuring is arranged in order to transfer personal wealth to the departing owner.

A programme of cash withdrawal from the business (to finance pension plans, life insurance policies, savings schemes, and so forth) may, in the long term, represent a significant drain on the firm's resources. On occasions it can seriously weaken company finances. Building up the balance sheet instead, however, itself exposes the owner to the risk that if the business suffers financial troubles at some stage in the future, the effects will spill over into his personal financial affairs.

There are no obvious right or wrong solutions here. Much will depend on the individual circumstances, in particular the cash flow and general resilience of the business concerned. If the business can accommodate it then, from the owner's point of view, a long-term cash withdrawal programme certainly offers three important advantages:

1. It protects the owner's personal wealth against business failure.
2. It enables the owner to spread his assets, freeing money for investment in a balanced and diversified portfolio.
3. The owner can maximise investment returns by switching between markets when opportunities arise.

It is, however, possible to adopt strategies that represent a middle course between the extremes of continuous cash withdrawal and building the balance sheet. A common example of this concerns business property.

The owner takes out a personal loan to finance the purchase of a property needed by the business, and then leases it to the business at a rental that hopefully is sufficient to repay the loan interest. The loan is secured on the owner's pension fund so that the capital will be repaid on retirement. A lot of owners actually set up their own property companies to enter into leasing agreements with the business. In the early stages, the arrangements are unlikely to be particularly profitable as the rental income is applied against interest payments. But after, say, five years and an upward rent review, the revenue position is likely to move into surplus and the capital value of the project becomes apparent. This capital value is being built up in favour of the owner directly, not the business.

This is just one illustration from a variety of techniques that can be employed to extract wealth from the family business in order to provide financial security for the owner before he relinquishes control. Other possibilities include, for example, the company buying-in some of the owner's shares, partial liquidations, and the sale of shares to children working in the business. There are so many options, all of which need to be tailored to individual and business circumstances, that it is not practical to undertake a detailed analysis here. Similarly, this is not the right place for a broadly based discussion of personal financial planning for family business owners. These two areas are fraught with complexity, and specialised assistance should be employed before making any decisions. Tax professionals, business consultants and personal financial planning experts can help owners to design a programme and approach that is right for them, their family, and their business.

SELLING THE BUSINESS

If the owner has no heirs willing (or able) to take over the family firm, or perhaps has insufficient funds, independent of the business, to provide for retirement, or if he has simply decided the time has come to start a new venture, then selling the business may be the best solution.

A difficult decision

While there may be cogent justification for selling, there may also be strong reasons why you should not sell (see Tables 9.1 and 9.2). You will have to carefully weigh up the importance of the arguments to reach what is likely to be a very tough decision.

A detached and logical approach, listing the pros and cons, will be helpful, but the process is also likely to raise some emotional dilemmas that you must be prepared to grapple with. Some entrepreneurs are able to start businesses, build them up, sell, and start all over again, taking a dispassionate view of the nature and results of their endeavours. For most owners, however, it is not that easy:

Table 9.1 *Some reasons for selling*

- Insufficient personal liquidity
- Need to finance retirement
- Economics – industry consolidation, for example
- A short-term business – it has achieved all it can
- Carrying on is too risky
- An excellent offer has been received
- No interest in the succession process on your part
- You are interested, but there is no successor
- Poor prognosis for family relationships
- Leadership loses interest
- 'To prove I can do what I want to do'

1. Along with the investment of money, time and energy across the years in establishing the business, you will also have made an emotional investment, the true extent of which may only become apparent when you come to consider selling.
2. Family businesses have unique and valuable characteristics, and these are likely to be under threat following a sale.
3. Many of the employees will also be close friends, and you may suffer feelings of betrayal if the company is sold – especially if it is sold to a competitor.
4. You may find it difficult to accept if the purchaser decides to radically alter your company – introduce a new corporate philosophy, reposition it in a different market sector, and so on.

It will sometimes be part of the deal that, once your business is sold, you and perhaps other key managers will continue to work for the acquiring company. It is tempting to believe that this will help to reduce the impact of some of these problems, but do not set your hopes too high. As you are wooed by the

Table 9.2 *Some reasons for not selling*

- The business is part of the family
- An important legacy
- Best long-term investment available
- Opportunity for the children
- Do not want the children to inherit a lot of cash
- The business is a flagship
- Important for the employees
- Something meaningful to do

buyers, many vague promises are likely to be made about the wonderful prospects and the fact that you will effectively stay in control but, at the end of the day, the buyers may view your employment contract as merely an extra on the purchase price.

Also, once the sale goes through, the bureaucratic culture of many large businesses is so alien to that of smaller family enterprises that owners generally find the transition extremely difficult and, not infrequently, impossible. Perhaps you will be able to sell your firm, fit into the new organisation, and enjoy a satisfying career. But it may be better not to count on it.

The mechanics of a sale
Finding a buyer, valuing the business, and negotiating the sale are all huge topics in their own right, and beyond the scope of this book. However, points to note and some broad guidelines include the following:

1. As regards finding a buyer, in a recent UK survey almost 90 per cent of family company respondents indicated that an approach had been received within the last six to seven years.
2. Despite what you may be told, there are no completely objective or scientific ways to value a business.
3. The negotiated price will represent a hybrid of many factors including asset value, earnings (both quantity

and quality), the growth rate and period, rate of
return, comparison with other companies, tax
considerations, and the market supply and demand of
companies for sale.
4. Negotiations are often best handled by someone other
than the owner. They should be planned for and not
treated casually.
5. Tax implications will have a profound effect on the
transaction, and it is vital to seek professional
assistance at an early stage.

The principal options

Broadly, there are four ways in which wealth tied up in the
business can be realised so that cash can be enjoyed in
retirement and, subsequently, by the family. These are:

- liquidating the business;
- a trade sale;
- stock market flotation; and
- a management buy-out.

Liquidation

In a members' voluntary liquidation, a liquidator is appointed
to sell off the company's assets, pay its debts and the liquidation
expenses, and distribute the cash surplus to shareholders. The
company is then dissolved.

The procedure tends to carry bankruptcy connotations, but it
is in fact a perfectly legitimate method of realising cash proceeds
from the business. It can be a viable option, especially in cases
that do not involve large closure costs and significant redun-
dancies. Generally, however, liquidation is unlikely to generate
as much money as selling the business as a going concern.

A trade sale

This is usually a more attractive proposition as far as most
entrepreneurs are concerned. Selling to purchasers within the
trade, who understand what your business is all about, will

often result in a better price than a sale to outsiders. In many cases, the owner may be able to receive a straightforward cash consideration and effectively wash his hands of the company at the date of sale. Structuring the sale agreement is inevitably complex, and great attention must be paid, among other things, to the terms of the warranties and indemnities requested by the purchaser.

Taxation considerations. Whether a company is sold or liquidated, advice should be sought to ensure the transaction is carried out in the most tax-efficient manner. In particular, following the closer alignment of income tax and capital gains tax rates, it is now often profitable to strip out wealth from the company through dividend payments prior to a sale. This is because dividends carry a tax credit in respect of advance corporation tax suffered by the company, whereas there is no similar form of tax deduction at source in respect of capital gains. The effective rate of tax on dividends is generally lower than the tax payable on capital gains. Consideration could be given to taking additional salary out of a company as it is tax deductible for corporation tax purposes, albeit taxable in the hands of the individual. Each case has to be considered on its own merits.

There are also tax advantages in selling as a going concern rather than selling off individual assets. These include:

1. Gains on the disposal, otherwise subject to capital gains tax, can be deferred if the sale is to a company in exchange for shares rather than cash. Depending on the particular circumstances, some consideration could be given to issuing loan notes.
2. No value added tax is payable on the sale if certain conditions are met.
3. Stamp duty is payable on the transfer of shares (by a person purchasing or receiving a gift of the shares) at the rate of 1 per cent of their market value. The rates of stamp duty on transfers of properties vary

depending on the consideration. Properties with consideration of over IR£60,000, for example, attract duty at 6 per cent.

4. Unused trading losses can be preserved.
5. Where other conditions are met, retirement relief should be available.

Generous reliefs from capital gains tax are available under the retirement relief rules where a shareholder disposes of an interest in his family trading company. The retirement relief provisions are complex but, broadly, the vendor must be aged over 55. If you meet the conditions for relief, currently the first IR£200,000 of the sale proceeds are wholly exempt from capital gains tax. There is a total exemption if the shares are transferred to children.

Going public

The owners of some companies can achieve personal liquidity and raise additional capital for the firm by way of a public flotation.

Any such firm needs to be a substantial operation for this option to be viable. In a study we conducted in September 1992, we found that small and medium-sized companies with a market capitalisation of less than IR£40–50 million (whether quoted on the Unlisted Securities Market or Official List) were experiencing severe difficulty in continuing to attract the institutional investment which had been a major source of funding for them in the past. This would indicate that a company would require annual profits (or have the ability to earn profits within the medium term once quoted) in excess of IR£3 million per annum to fully benefit from a stock exchange quotation.

Stock market sentiment must also be favourable, and current indications are that the 1980s boom conditions in the UK and Irish new issues sector are unlikely to return for some time.

It is also important to emphasise that it is difficult for entrepreneurs to float their firms with a view to retirement. Not surprisingly, the market's assessment of public offerings centres on the issuer's prospects and investment potential. Companies coming to the market simply to provide an exit route for retiring founder shareholders are unlikely to meet with a rapturous reception. It is, therefore, essential to build up a good management team (family or otherwise) so that the founding shareholder can sell shares without causing too much concern.

The main advantages of going public are as follows:

- The opportunity to raise new money for the business (both when the firm goes public and subsequently) by the issue of new shares.
- Shares in the company (instead of cash and borrowings) can be used as consideration for acquisitions.
- Enhanced status for the company, a higher profile for its products or services, and an improved credit rating.
- The opportunity for the owners to realise part, or all, of their investment, either at the time of the flotation or subsequently, and to establish a market value for their retained shareholdings.
- The provision of a ready market for shares held by family members.

The principal disadvantages of a public flotation are:

- Accountability to outside shareholders is often not welcomed by owners.
- Pressure can be placed on management to ensure the quality of short-term performance at the expense of the long-term best interests of the company.
- Disclosure requirements are significant, and confidentiality no longer attaches to financial and other information about the company.
- Vulnerability to an unwelcome takeover bid is increased, dependent on the percentage of the company's capital in public hands.
- Possible personal taxation liabilities for any vendor

shareholder and a higher market value for retained shares (for example, in the event of the death of a shareholder).
- The expenses of going public, as well as the probable increase in ongoing costs arising from greater administrative formalities and the need for the company's reporting function to be strengthened.

Careful consideration should be given to the decision whether or not to float. No two companies are the same and there is no right or wrong for every situation. Some family businesses find that going public is highly advantageous and provides an answer to most of the problems they wanted to resolve. Others, however, discover that the adverse aspects of the move can be significant, as evidenced by the recent steady trickle of listed companies seeking to return to the private sector.

A management buy-out

As successful family firms grow, the core team that founded the business is often reinforced by other managers – brought in from outside, family members, or promoted employees. There comes a time when you should be able to step back and let them run the business, so why not consider selling it to them? When family members are part of the management, a management buy-out represents, in some respects, a compromise between transferring the shares to the family and an outright trade sale.

A management buy-out can provide solutions to a number of problems:

- The owner realises cash.
- The management team acquires an even greater incentive to make the business prosper.
- The business is likely to keep its identity, sparing the owner some of the moral dilemmas involved in a sale to an outside organisation, discussed earlier.
- Actual and potential conflicts between family and non-family managers should be resolved.

At the same time, however, there are two important difficulties associated with management buy-outs. First, during the capital raising exercise to finance the acquisition, your managers will devote a lot of their energies to talking to venture capitalists, drafting prospectuses, and preparing institutional presentations, and there is a risk that they will cease to pay proper attention to managing the business. Even if they succeed in raising the finance, it is possible that your company (and what it is worth) will have suffered in the process.

Secondly, if the managers fail to raise the money, you end up in the position you started from except that you have a team of managers who have been distracted from their work for months, and who are now disappointed and disgruntled because their hopes and ambitions have been dashed.

The price you can expect to receive for the business also has a double-edged aspect. Part of the recent popularity of management buy-outs has been attributed to the fact that a loyal management team, thoroughly *au fait* with the business, is likely to pay more for the company than a wary, cost-conscious outsider with years of acquisitions experience. On the other hand, some management buy-outs fail because the management knows the business *too well*, and is unwilling to try and come up with anything like the asking price.

SHARE PURCHASE AGREEMENTS

Especially in cases of multiple family ownership (i.e. generally in the third generation and beyond), family business tensions are often caused by too many participants with differing backgrounds, objectives and viewpoints. An effective way to limit the number of owners, as mentioned in previous chapters, is to establish a share purchase agreement.

Such agreements provide for the mandatory purchase by the surviving shareholder of another shareholder's interest if the latter dies first. Clearly, it is best to establish such agreements at a time when the participants are all healthy and nobody knows who will be the first to die. It is generally in the survivor's best interests to secure ownership of the shares involved, while the deceased's family is usually better off with cash. Family members who are not going to be active in the business tend to prefer income-producing assets to a minority interest in a private company that may well not pay dividends.

Also, share purchase agreements giving the company and/or the family the right of first refusal before any shares can be sold, allow owners to limit significantly the opportunities for outside investors to purchase an interest in the company.

Relinquishing control: Key suggestions

- Building financial security is an important element in the owner's preparations for a successful retirement. This can be achieved either inside or outside the business, or by selling it.
- Many owners neglect their own finances. Employ a personal financial adviser as well as a business tax consultant to help you plan for retirement.
- Be prepared for the fact that selling the family business may be more of an emotional wrench than you anticipate.
- While some owners can be happy as the employee of the new owner, most find the cultures incompatible and the loss of ultimate control unacceptable.
- You may not be the best person to negotiate the sale of your business. Consider employing a professional.
- Depending on your circumstances, important personal and commercial objectives may be attained by selling through a liquidation, trade sale, flotation or management buy-out. In considering any of these options, professional help is essential.
- Share purchase agreements can be used to resolve many of the complications that result from multiple family ownership of a business.

---

10 Passing Down the Business

Passing down ownership of the family business to the next generation, without incurring huge tax liabilities, requires careful and detailed planning. So too does accomplishing the transfer without triggering family disputes. The process is an emotionally sensitive one and has the potential to pit parents against children, or siblings against each other.

In Chapter 9, methods were discussed for the owner to dispose of his interest in the business, and to realise cash, during his lifetime. In this chapter, the concern centres on ways that the family company can most effectively be gifted or bequeathed to the owner's heirs. The lessening of estate tax burdens over recent years has tended to favour continued family ownership of firms. Owners of family companies can substantially reduce or delay the tax payable when the business is passed on, but this does require forward planning. As early as possible, you need to decide on your long-term objectives, and to use lifetime gifts or trusts to pass on ownership tax efficiently. Key questions will include:

- Who is to own shares in my business in the next generation?
- Who, either individually or together, should have control of the company?
- Can equity ownership and voting control be separated?
- How can I guarantee financial security for my spouse?

- How can I be fair, and be seen to be fair, to my heirs?
- Does treating the children fairly mean that I must distribute shares and voting rights equally among them?
- What is the best way to organise my affairs so that my heirs are not burdened by estate taxes, and to safeguard their ability to carry on running the business effectively?

ESTATE PLANNING PRINCIPLES

Implicit in these questions, and regardless of which techniques and tools are used in estate planning, there are three guiding principles that must always be taken into account: continuity of the business; liquidity; and family needs.

1. *Continuity.* Effective management of a family company must provide for continuity. The main eventualities that should be planned for are disability, retirement and death, and, of the three, only retirement can be planned within a predetermined time frame. The most critical factor in preserving the family's business assets is to avoid the forced sale of the firm.
2. *Liquidity.* The departure, for whatever reason, of a principal in a family business can create sudden demands for cash to pay taxes, family support, or to provide retirement income. Effective planning requires estimates of the family's future needs and the means to provide for them, including the necessary liquid resources to cover the payment of personal estate taxes.
3. *Family needs.* Evaluating the financial needs of the family, as well as their future role in the business, is the most important part of estate planning. The financial well-being of each family member must be kept in mind, including contingencies such as birth, death, marriage and marriage breakdown. In considering the family's future relationship with the

business it will be necessary to address the question of 'What is fair?'

Treating heirs fairly

Disputes and grudges over inheritance provide a plentiful supply of family conflicts, and this is especially so when a business is involved. Social rules dictate that wealth should, in the absence of powerful reasons to the contrary, be passed on to the next generation under arrangements that can broadly be described as fair. But fairness is a particularly subjective concept, and its application to passing down the family business is likely to be the source of an almost infinite variety of interpretations.

Often, the main cause of trouble is the assumption that fairness means equality of treatment. But applying this idea to a family company is generally destructive and dangerous. Some of the children will be better able to manage the business than others; the eldest child may not be the best businessman; and some of the children may already be working in the business, while others may have absolutely no interest in it.

Another difficulty surrounds the conflict of interest between heirs who are active in the business and those who are not. For example, active members will generally take a conservative approach to the company's money, ploughing profits back and investing in order to make the firm stronger, more resilient, and more competitive. Passive members, on the other hand, are likely to give a higher priority to money paid out by the firm in the form of dividends on their shares.

This conflict can lead to more bitter disagreements about rewards. Active shareholders will be quick to point out that it is they who do all the hard work and suffer the sleepless nights (in return, they will often argue, for ridiculously low salary and benefit levels), while their passive counterparts sit back and do little or nothing, except campaign to bleed the company of every penny it has in cash. The passive members will respond that the active members are grossly overpaid – company cars, pension plans, 'and what about that all expenses paid holiday in the Seychelles as part of a so-called sales conference?' – and so on.

You can go a long way to reducing the scope for this sort of turmoil by thinking through the potential problems in advance, and sharing your thinking with your heirs. They are more likely to accept perceived inequalities if they understand what you are trying to achieve. You may well have to depart from the principle of equality and bequeath shares in the business to selected heirs, and you may have to treat heirs who are active in the business differently from those who are not. It is rarely possible to satisfy everyone, but if you can discuss the issues and explain your difficulties and objectives, at least you may be able to avoid the bitterness that can result from misunderstandings.

The conflict of interest between active and passive share-holders can also be mitigated by constructive estate planning options, based on a clear appreciation of the distinction between ownership and control of the family firm in the next generation.

OWNERSHIP AND CONTROL CONSIDERATIONS

Ordinary shares in a company generally carry three basic entitlements – the right to an equity interest in the business, the right to vote and the right to receive dividends. If possible, the ideal method of passing down the family company is to bequeath the shares to the active members, and other assets to the inactive members. If, however, the business represents most of the value in the owner's estate, this may not be practical and it will be necessary to consider other options that at least provide the active members with voting control (the significance of various levels of shareholding interest is set out in Table 10.1).

There are various methods of isolating voting and equity ownership rights, and these will be discussed later. First, however, there are some alternative courses of action that should not be overlooked.

Life insurance
A life insurance policy in favour of named beneficiaries can be used to provide cash for the heirs who are not to be active in the business. The amount of money they receive under the policy

Table 10.1 *Significant company voting rights*

Shareholding	Comments
80% or more	In most circumstances, can facilitate the compulsory acquisition of 100% of all shares of the particular class in issue in the event of an offer to take over the company.
75% or more	Confers the right to pass special resolutions and provides overall control of the company. Also can exempt the board of directors from compliance with pre-emption rights in relation to the issue of new shares.
Over 50%	Confers the right (a) to appoint and remove directors and accordingly provides effective control of the management of the company; (b) to authorise the board of directors to issue shares for cash subject to pre-emption rights under which such shares must be allotted pro rata to the shareholdings of existing members; (c) to authorise the board of a public limited company to make market purchases of its own shares; (d) to approve a director's service contract for a period exceeding five years (terminable by the company only in specified circumstances; and (e) to approve an arrangement between the company and a director

Contd. over

Table 10.1 (contd.)

Shareholding	Comments
	(or connected person) in relation to the acquisition or disposal of non-cash assets exceeding IR£50,000 or 10% of the company's 'relevant assets', as defined.
Over 25%	Confers the right to block special resolutions such as are required for members' voluntary winding-up, the alteration of the memorandum and articles of association or to dispense with pre-emption rights on the issue of shares for cash.
Over 20%	In most circumstances, can prevent the compulsory acquisition of 100% of shares of the particular class in issue in the event of a takeover offer.
10% or more	Confers the right to requisition a general meeting of the members of the company pursuant to Section 132 of the Companies Act, 1963. However small the percentage holding, every shareholder has the right to avoid oppression from the majority shareholders.

can be made roughly equivalent to the value of shares bequeathed to the active members.

It may be possible to take out a 'key-man' insurance policy to provide the necessary funds for the company to purchase its own shares. A 'buy-back' arrangement can be put in place where the company will buy the shares from the estate of the deceased. The surviving shareholders retain control of the company as the deceased's shares are bought back by the company and cancelled. The dependants of the deceased shareholder can realise their shares for cash – and there will usually be no capital gains tax on this disposal as the shares will be acquired at market value at the date of death.

Share purchase agreements
Another approach to the problem involves bequeathing the shares to both active and inactive members, but imposing ownership conditions via a private share purchase agreement. Such an agreement can stipulate, for example, that inactive members are required to sell their shares to the active members (thus avoiding the sort of conflict that can arise between those who own the business and those who run it, illustrated in the case study on C&J Clark that followed Chapter 3). Bargaining and potential disagreements between siblings about the value of shares can be avoided if you include a clear formula for price calculation in the agreement.

Share purchase agreements can also provide a clear-cut solution to a number of other sensitive family business issues. Some companies, for example, restrict share ownership to bloodline family members, and enforce this through agreements that give the family first refusal before shareholdings may be transferred or sold. Similarly, a family member's involvement in marriage breakdown can be made to trigger a compulsory offer of their shares to the family.

Share purchase agreements, therefore, can provide an effective method of limiting both the number of owners and the opportunities for outside, potentially hostile investors to purchase an interest in the company.

Isolating voting control
If it is not practical to pass down all the shares in the family business to the active members, restricted voting shares may provide a means by which you can at least leave them with

voting control. It is possible to divide the company's share capital into two classes: only one class carries full voting rights, while the other is subject to voting restrictions (e.g. 100 shares represents one vote) or, indeed, carries no voting rights at all. This division then enables you to bequeath voting shares to heirs whom you wish to control the firm, and restricted voting shares to the others. This is a practical solution and confers no taxation benefits.

IMPLEMENTING THE ESTATE PLAN

Inheritance and other tax liabilities on the transfer of shares in the family business can cause severe problems in the absence of adequate planning. This section is intended only as an introduction and an overview to the wide variety of estate planning options. It is not a detailed tax guide and, because of the complexities and the unique circumstances and needs of each family business, specialised assistance should always be employed before making any decisions.

Trusts and their uses

A trust is essentially a device that enables you to give property to another person or institution to administer for the benefit of a third party or group. Until the mid-1970s, trusts enabled firms to be passed on in a flexible way to the next generation. They also facilitated the passing on of property in a tax-efficient manner, but subsequent fiscal legislation removed most of their advantages and, indeed, in some cases created tax problems. So be sure to obtain professional advice before embarking on the trust route.

As regards taxation, capital gains tax (discussed in more detail below) applies to property moving into or out of a trust. Generally, income received in a trust is subject to income tax at the standard rate. In addition, any income not distributed within a specified time limit is subject to a 20 per cent surcharge. Additionally, for certain discretionary trusts, there is a one-off

3 per cent charge on the value of the assets put into the trust, and an annual 1 per cent charge thereafter.

The person who provides the trust property and usually sets up the trust is known as the 'settlor'. The settlor transfers the ownership of property to trustees who hold it for the benefit of the beneficiaries. It is possible for the settlor to be one of the trustees and one of the beneficiaries. The terms of a trust can be extremely flexible, allowing the trustees to increase the class of beneficiaries and appoint capital back to the settlor. Most trusts can be divided into one of four categories:

1. A life interest trust – also known as an interest in possession trust. This is a trust where one or more persons have the right to receive the income from the trust property. This right can be for life or for a fixed period of time.
2. A bare trust, which can be 'looked through' directly to the beneficiary.
3. A discretionary trust. With this type of trust, no person has the right to the trust income; it is for the trustees to decide on the distribution of income and capital.
4. A discretionary will trust. This is the most common form of trust used nowadays in Ireland. In effect, the owner draws up a discretionary will trust during his lifetime, particularly where there are children below the age of 21 years who might inherit substantial wealth. The trust does not come into existence until the death of the settlor.

Gifting shares into a trust may provide a solution, for example, if the family business owner is concerned to retain control over major policy decisions affecting the company. The significance of various levels of shareholding interest is set out in Table 10.1. If, for instance, the share capital is divided equally between the donor and his brother, and he gifts one share to his daughter, then voting control could shift to his brother if his daughter decides to vote with her uncle on an issue affecting the company. On the other hand, if the gift is to a life interest or a discretionary trust, then the donor may be able to pass wealth to the family while effectively retaining control of the company. The family advantages of creating the trust may well outweigh the additional tax costs.

Another advantage of trusts is that all the shares can be gifted as a block to be held for the benefit of, say, three or four children. The division of shares between them need not take place until much later. This might be appropriate, for example, if the children are very young and it is not clear which of them will join the business. A discretionary trust settlement might be the best solution here. Additionally, the trustees will ensure that income is appointed out to the beneficiaries (including minors), thus allowing them to avail of their personal allowances and the tax bands.

Turning now to the wider issues relevant to implementing the estate plan, a material problem associated with the handing down or disposal of the family business is taxation. The main taxes that have to be considered are capital acquisitions tax (CAT), probate tax, capital gains tax (CGT) and stamp duty.

Capital acquisitions tax
CAT covers both gifts and inheritances, and relates to any gifts received after 28th February, 1974 and any inheritances received after 1st April, 1975. In general, it is the donee or beneficiary who has to pay the tax.

There is a territorial limit to the extent to which gifts and inheritances are taxable: usually, these rules mean that an Irish person and Irish assets are exposed to CAT. The technical rules stipulate that all the assets comprised in the gift or inheritance are taxable, where, at the time of the gift or inheritance, the disponer (the person making the gift/inheritance) is domiciled in Ireland, or the proper law of the disposition is Irish. Otherwise, only assets situated in Ireland are chargeable. There are various tax-free thresholds between the disponer and a beneficiary depending on their relationship. For 1993, these thresholds are as follows:

- IR£171,750
  — from parent to child
  — from child to parent for inheritance only
- IR£22,900
  — from blood relatives: 'relatives' include parents (for gifts), siblings, uncles, aunts
- IR£11,450
  — all others.

It is important to note that these thresholds are indexed on an annual basis in line with the Consumer Price Index.

CAT is calculated by aggregating all gifts and inheritances received since 2nd June, 1982, deducting any relevant exemptions, and then applying the following tax rates: IR£10,000 at 20 per cent; IR£40,000 at 30 per cent; IR£50,000 at 35 per cent; and the balance at 40 per cent.

The practical difference between a gift and an inheritance is that, while the tax on a gift and the tax on an inheritance are both calculated using the same table of tax rates, the tax so calculated on a gift is reduced by 25 per cent provided the disponer survives for two years after making the gift.

Transfers between spouses are exempt from inheritance tax and from gift tax.

Probate tax
There is a 2 per cent probate tax on all estates in excess of IR£10,000 (excluding the family home where the spouse is the successor).

Capital gains tax
CGT arises on a disposal of an asset or a deemed disposal and, generally, the tax is calculated on the open market value of the asset. The tax rate is 40 per cent, irrespective of the period of ownership.

There are two main areas where CGT may arise in relation to the disposal of a family business: gifting between family members, which is a deemed disposal and crystallises a CGT charge; and retirement relief, which does not.

Generally, a gift between family members is considered a deemed disposal at market value. Therefore, the person making the disposal will have an exposure to CGT on the deemed market value of the shares less the original cost of the shares as indexed for inflation and the annual personal exemption of IR£2000 for a married person or IR£1000 for a single person.

Retirement relief
If an individual (meeting certain criteria) makes a disposal to his children, the transaction is exempt from CGT irrespective of the consideration. This is referred to as 'retirement relief'.

Broadly speaking, retirement relief from CGT is granted on the sale of specified business assets by an individual who is aged 55 years or more. It is not dependent upon retirement as such. Where the business is being disposed of to the taxpayer's children, there is no limit on the sale price, or gain, which may qualify for the relief. If the sale is to others, a limit of IR£200,000 is placed on the proceeds qualifying for relief. Retirement relief is available in respect of disposals of 'qualifying assets'. These are defined as:

- Chargeable business assets of the individual, which he has owned for a period of not less than 10 years ending with the date of disposal. 'Chargeable business assets' are assets used for the purposes of a trade, farming, a profession, or an office or an employment carried out by the individual.
- Shares or securities owned by an individual for a period of not less than 10 years ending with the date of disposal, being shares or securities in a trading or farming company which has also been that individual's family company for not less that the 10-year period. It is also essential that the individual has been a full-time working

director of the company for a period of not less than five years.

For the purposes of the latter provision, 'family company' is defined as a company where the individual holds either 25 per cent or more of the voting rights, or holds 10 per cent or more of the voting rights where he and his family together hold 75 per cent or more of such rights. 'Family' includes spouse, relatives and relatives of the spouse. It is important to note that the child must retain the shares for 10 years, otherwise the tax which the parent should have paid becomes payable by the child, together with any CGT attaching to the later disposal.

In relation to any assets which do not attract retirement relief, obviously CGT is payable even though no cash may be passing.

Another important relieving section which may be important for some family firms is that where gift tax or inheritance tax is charged on an event, and that same event constitutes a disposal for CGT purposes. In these circumstances, any CGT due is allowed as a credit against the gift or inheritance tax.

Valuation

The quantum of the tax charge will depend on the valuation of the company at the time it is transferred. There are numerous ways of valuing a company, but in general it will be valued at the higher of:

- a breakup basis; or
- a multiple of post-tax profits (ranging between about five to nine times); or
- a mixture of these criteria.

Obviously, various areas have to be addressed in applying these valuation criteria – for example, the age of the proprietor, the proprietor's involvement, the value of the business as a going concern, etc. The final valuation for tax purposes must be agreed with the Revenue Commissioners. If a substantial gift or estate is involved, it is essential to obtain professional advice because valuation can become a contest, with the Revenue Commissioners claiming a high value and the taxpayer a low value.

Special rules apply for valuing shares in a private family company which, following receipt of the gift or the inheritance, is a company 'controlled' by the beneficiary and his relatives. The effect of this provision is that shares in a family company which is trading are to be valued on an open market basis, as if they formed part of a parcel of shares owned by the beneficiary and his relatives – i.e. as a majority shareholding without discount for minority interests.

The benefits of life insurance

There are basically two methods of dealing with a potential charge to inheritance tax. The first is to maximise lifetime gifts and to utilise the available reliefs and exemptions. However, although this planning will reduce the tax charge, it is unlikely to be fully mitigated. The second approach, therefore, is based on the acceptance of an ultimate tax charge and uses life assurance as a way of providing funds for the beneficiaries so that they can meet the tax liability. A combination of both methods will generally be used in an effective estate plan.

But life insurance can also provide a solution to a range of other family business issues discussed elsewhere in this book. It can, for example:

- Help to fund family share purchase agreements.
- Finance cash legacies to heirs who are not active in the business so that shares in the company can be passed down to active heirs.
- Guarantee the financial security of a surviving spouse.
- Provide money to help offset the loss to the business resulting from the owner's death. This is called 'key-man' insurance and it can protect the company's capital base by covering, for example, the repayment of loans and overdrafts. A key-man policy can also provide funds for the company to purchase its own shares.
- Enable surviving shareholders, via cross-life policies, to

finance the purchase of shares in the business from the deceased's estate.

It is also possible to take out what's called a 'Section 60 policy' to cover the tax arising on a gift or an inheritance. The main benefit of these policies is that the proceeds do not form part of the estate in so far as they are used to discharge the tax liability.

CONCLUSIONS

It has not been practical in this chapter to provide more than a broad overview of the philosophy of estate planning for family business people, the important considerations that should guide their thinking, and an introduction to the main tools and techniques for implementing an estate plan. Everything rests on the particular circumstances of the individual, the family, and the business. With complex and rapidly changing tax laws, this is a highly specialised area and it is vital that you take advantage of professional estate planning advice.

However, the important message that this brief summary has tried to highlight is that enormous opportunities exist for creating flexible and tax-efficient estate planning structures. The key point is that if an estate plan has been carefully thought out, in good time, and has been properly implemented, then the death of the owner of a family firm should never require the sale of business assets to meet tax liabilities.

Passing down the business: Key suggestions

- Owners of family businesses can substantially reduce or delay tax liabilities payable when the business is passed on, but this does require careful forward planning.
- Continuity of the business, liquidity, and family needs are the corner-stones of estate planning.

Key suggestions (contd.)

- Ensuring that ownership of the business ends up in the right hands in the next generation may require treating heirs differently depending on whether or not they are active in the business, and passing on voting control to selected heirs.
- Talk to your heirs and explain to them what it is you are trying to achieve with your estate plan.
- Minimise estate taxes through the use of lifetime gifts and trust settlements. Any residual liability can be funded through life insurance.

Case Histories

THE IMPORTANCE OF
CHOOSING THE RIGHT SUCCESSOR

This case concerns a substantial dress manufacturing business based in Hong Kong and Ireland. The firm was extremely successful under the guiding hand of its founder, a dynamic entrepreneur who was able to manage not only the fashion side of the business but also its finances and administration.

The time came when he needed help in continuing to run the company but, because he had married quite late in life, his children were still young and there was no obvious successor. He therefore persuaded his nephew, a trained barrister, to join the firm, insisting he spend time learning about the business. Shortly after this, the founder suddenly died.

The nephew soon found himself out of his depth but, even though an opportunity arose to sell the business, he refused because he would not have benefited from a sale. He continued for a number of years to resist family pressure to sell until the company was eventually forced into insolvent liquidation.

This straightforward case highlights the importance of taking the greatest care when choosing a successor. The founder here had the choice of introducing outside management or taking on a family member. He chose the latter, to the long-term detriment of the business.

A SON BUYING SHARES FROM THE FAMILY

This example is about an individual, in his mid-30s, who was experiencing enormous frustration trying to run the family business in the face of constant interference from his parents who had spent many years building up the company.

The son expressed his worries that he was not able to function effectively within the business because he did not have a clear mandate from his parents. The parents, for their part, were reluctant to empower the son because the business represented the bulk of their personal wealth and they were worried that a deterioration in profits would adversely affect their retirement.

A plan was therefore devised under which the son formed a new company (in which he owned all the shares), and the parents then gifted to him 60 per cent of their equity in the family business. Following this, the new company took a bank loan (secured mainly on the underlying business assets) to enable it to purchase his parents' remaining 40 per cent interest. Subsequently, a share exchange took place and the new company was left owning 100 per cent of the family business. The net result was that the son acquired complete control of the business while his parents received sufficient cash, after tax, to provide financial security for their retirement.

Once the parents had made a decision on precisely what amount of money they needed in the bank in order to allay their worries and to avoid future claims on the business, it was a simple question of mechanics to put a structure in place that would achieve the objectives of both sides.

This approach can be applied quite often. Children should not be worried about the principle of borrowing money in this way if it achieves both a sound basis for their parents' retirement and also clears a way for the future development of the business.

THE BRIDGE

A specialist manufacturing company, formed in the late-1940s, was founded and run by an autocratic genius. Nothing happened at the factory which he did not know about, and he carried all the management procedures and performance figures in his head.

The company prospered under his control, although it was still something of a one-man business, until, in the late-1970s, the founder died very suddenly. He had two sons who were involved in the business, and two daughters who were not. The sons represented the eldest and the youngest of his four children, but neither was prepared to take over as the new MD. This task was therefore given to the general manager, who had been with the firm since it began, and who acted as a 'bridge' between the two generations of the founding family.

A few years went by, with both sons continuing to work in the business, and eventually the point was reached at which the family felt able to resume control. It happened at a convenient time, with the bridge deciding to retire, allowing the younger son to take over as MD and the older son to become chairman. Subsequent to this management reorganisation, the family has retained control of the business, which has enjoyed dramatic growth.

The case illustrates that the judicious use of a bridge can represent a very useful compromise between succession by family members who may be unqualified or unprepared for the role, and the formal introduction of outside management. It also highlights the importance of planning for succession. The founder here had not addressed the question and, as a result, the family was left to sort it out after the event.

SUCCESSION AND BEYOND

This company, a specialist manufacturer, was established in the late-1940s.

The owner had four children, three girls and a boy, and was very keen that his son should succeed him in the business in due course.

Following advice in the mid-1970s, 50 per cent of the shares were transferred to the son and the remaining 50 per cent to th

3 daughters jointly. The son was made chairman and chief executive of the company.

This seemingly sensible arrangement actually placed the son under enormous strain as a result of a conflict of interest. His sisters were exposed to a financial gamble concerning his ability to run the company properly. How could he manage the firm on a truly commercial footing – taking risks, starting new ventures, borrowing money, and so on – when the business was half-owned by his sisters? These conflicts placed the son in an invidious position and, by mutual agreement, it was therefore decided that the sisters should dispose of their interest in the business.

As well as shares in the company, the siblings also owned the freehold of the firm's main premises. A scheme was devised whereby the son purchased the shares from his sisters, thus giving him effective control. At the same time, the firm also bought the freehold property. As a result of careful planning, neither transaction gave rise to a tax liability, and the scheme resulted in half of the company's distributable reserves being passed, in cash, to the sisters.

Some time later, it became clear to the son that the business was in a declining market and he decided to sell the group's principal operating subsidiary. In an effort to ensure fairness to all the parties concerned, the original purchase arrangements had included a stipulation that in the event of the future sale of part of the company, any increase in value should be passed in the form of additional consideration to the sisters. As things turned out, however, the sale of the subsidiary took place at approximately the same valuation that applied under the scheme, and no further payments were necessary.

This is a case of an individual who recognised the commercial sense in making a disposal, and not holding on to a company for emotional reasons. He had to then decide what to do with the ˉˉˉˉˉˉˉ by the sale – but that was a separate problem!

Simpson Xavier

PUBLICATIONS

Unless otherwise indicated, all publications are available from Simpson Xavier free of charge.

Client service brochures
Taxation Services
Corporate Finance
Corporate Recovery and Insolvency Services
Consultancy Services
Systems for the Financial Services Sector

Technical publications
The Horwath International Tax Planning Manual, *published by CCH, IR£250.00*
Tax Data Card, Annual, File

Surveys
Review of the Dublin USM, *IR£50.00*

Simpson Xavier Horwath Consulting publications
Technical publications
Irish Hotel Industry Review, *IR£50.00*
Horwath Book of Tourism, *published by Macmillan, IR£40.00*
Hotel Accounts and Their Audit, *published by ICAEW, IR£25.00*
Hotels of the Future: Strategies and Action Plan, *International Hotel Association, Summary Report IR£40.00, Full Report IR£250.00*
Uniform System of Accounts for Restaurants, *published by AHMA, IR£10.00*
Uniform System of Accounts for Hotels, *published by AHMA, IR£16.00*

SERVICES OF THE FIRM

Accountancy and audit
Accounting services
Company secretarial
Family business unit
Financial planning
Specialised audits
Statutory audits

Financial advice
Corporate disposals
Corporate finance &
  investigations
Entertainment industry
  advisory services
Litigation support
Personal financial planning
Property industry
Raising finance
Trust management
Venture & development
  capital

Tax
Business Expansion Scheme
Corporate taxation
International tax planning
Personal taxation
Remuneration/benefits
  planning
Tax investigations
Irish tax planning
VAT planning

Corporate recovery and insolvency
Bankruptcies

Corporate recovery & viability
  studies
Examinerships
Investigations
Liquidations
Receiverships
Voluntary arrangements

Consultancy services
Charities
Computer systems: design,
  selection & system
  implementation
Corporate strategy
European business unit
Executive search
Executive selection
Expert witnesses (tribunals
  etc.)
Feasibility studies
Franchising services
Government grants
Human resource services
Management training
Marketing studies
Organisation reviews
Project management
Property consulting
Relocation services
Remuneration planning
Strategic planning
Public sector information
  technology
Tribunal/arbitration experts
Total quality management
Treasury management

Horwath Consulting
*Specialist advice to the hotel,
tourism and leisure
industries*
Market & financial feasibility
studies
Project appraisal
Strategic planning
National & regional tourism
planning
Marketing & promotional
strategies
Financial planning
Management accounting,
control & reporting
Operational reviews & profit
improvement studies
Manpower planning/training
Executive selection
Planning enquiries,
arbitration & legal support

OFFICES

Dublin
Simpson Xavier Court
20 Merchants Quay
Dublin 8
Tel: (01) 6790022
Fax: (01) 6790111
Contact: *Philip Smyth*

Limerick
Four Michael Street
Limerick
Tel: (061) 414455
Fax: (061) 414172
Contact: *Brian McGann*

Associated Office
Stoy Hayward
Lindsey House
10 Callender Street
Belfast BT1 5BN
Tel: (080232) 439009
Fax: (080232) 439010
Contact: *Jim Orme*

INTERNATIONAL OFFICES
Andorra
Argentina
Australia
Austria
Bahrain
Belgium
Bermuda
Bolivia
Botswana
Brazil
Canada
Cayman Islands
Channel Islands
Chile
Colombia
Cyprus
Denmark
Dominican Republic
Egypt
Ethiopia
Fiji
Finland
France
Germany
Greece
Guatemala

Haiti	New Zealand
Hong Kong	Nigeria
Hungary	Norway
Iceland	Pakistan
India	Panama
Indonesia	Philippines
Israel	Portugal
Italy	Saudi Arabia
Jamaica	Singapore
Japan	South Africa
Kenya	Spain
Korea	Sri Lanka
Lebanon	Sweden
Luxembourg	Switzerland
Malaysia	Taiwan
Malta	Thailand
Mexico	Turkey
Monaco	United Arab Emirates
Morocco	United Kingdom
Nepal	Venezuela
Netherlands	Zimbabwe